The South Africa GLUTEN-FREE
COOKBOOK

The South African
GLUTEN-FREE
COOKBOOK

Published in 2017 by Struik Lifestyle, an imprint of Penguin Random House South Africa (Pty) Ltd
Company Reg. No. 1953/000441/07
The Estuaries, 4 Oxbow Crescent, Century Avenue, Century City 7441, Cape Town, South Africa
PO Box 1144, Cape Town, 8000, South Africa
www.penguinrandomhouse.co.za

PUBLISHER: Linda de Villiers
MANAGING EDITOR: Cecilia Barfield
DESIGN MANAGER: Beverley Dodd
DESIGNER: Helen Henn
EDITOR & INDEXER: Gill Gordon
PHOTOGRAPHER: Myburgh du Plessis
STYLIST: Sarah Dall
STYLIST'S ASSISTANT: Esme Retief
PROOFREADER: Bronwen Maynier

Reproduction: Hirt & Carter Cape (Pty) Ltd
Printed and bound in China by RR Donnelley Asia Printing Solutions Ltd.

ISBN 978-1-43230-651-9

Contents

Introduction

This book contains a collection of tried-and-tested recipes, which may prove useful when following a gluten-free lifestyle. But please remember that it is not an approved nutritional or dietary guide. If you are unwell or suspect you may have coeliac disease or gluten intolerance, seek professional advice from a doctor or qualified dietitian. And remember; gluten-free recipes are not necessarily healthier than similar recipes containing gluten. Many gluten-free flours are just as refined and high in carbohydrates as regular flour.

What is gluten? Gluten is composed of two proteins – gliadin and glutenin – which occur in wheat, barley, spelt and rye. Glutenin, a large, loosely coiled protein, provides most of the strength and elasticity in dough. Gliadin, which is much smaller and more tightly coiled, provides the stretch in dough. When these proteins are mixed with water, their respective molecules link up with each other to form long elastic chains, called gluten.

Where does gluten occur? It is important to read the labels on all packaged and processed food. Gluten is found in products you might never have imagined contained wheat, like salad dressings, marinades, sauces and gravies, as well as sweets like liquorice. Spices, seasonings and powdered soups may contain gluten in the form of ingredients used to prevent 'clumping'. Processed meats, sausages and burgers may be bulked out with breadcrumbs or wheat-based 'fillers', while frozen chips are often coated with a fine layer of flour. Even alcoholic drinks can contain gluten: beer is made from barley, maize and/or other grains. Many cosmetics and lipsticks contain gluten, as do some medicines and supplements. 'Wheat-free' does not necessarily mean 'gluten-free'. Grains like barley, spelt and rye may be wheat-free, but they are not gluten-free.

Coeliac disease The most common reason to follow a gluten-free diet is to treat coeliac disease. Often referred to as an allergy or intolerance, it is an autoimmune disease that occurs when the body's immune system reacts abnormally to gluten and produces antibodies that attack its own tissue. As a result, the villi lining the small intestine become unable to absorb nutrients, and sufferers can become malnourished. Not everyone who has a gluten intolerance develops coeliac disease. However, many people display a sensitivity to gluten that ranges from mild to severe. This is called non-coeliac gluten sensitivity.

Baking without gluten A mixture of flours generally works best for baking. Pre-mixed gluten-free flour is available from health stores or supermarkets, but many of the recipes in this book have been tested using the gluten-free flour mix on page 8. For convenience, make up a batch the flour mix and store it in an airtight container. Milk powder, which contains protein, helps with the structure, tenderness and browning of baked goods and adds a richness of flavour. However, if you follow a dairy-free diet, you can just leave it out.

Gluten-free flour mix

500 g white rice flour

350 g brown rice flour

200 g potato flour/starch

150 g tapioca flour/starch

50 ml (30 g) fat-free milk powder

10 ml xanthan gum

1. Combine all the ingredients in a bowl and use a wire whisk to blend well. Store in an airtight container and use as necessary.

Notes • *We use the gluten-free flour mix in many recipes in this book. Where 'gluten-free flour mix' is specified, the recipe has been tested using this mix. If a recipe calls for 'gluten-free flour', you can use either the flour mix, a single gluten-free flour (see below), or a mixture of gluten-free flours that you can blend yourself, or buy.*

• *When calculating quantities, remember that 150 g flour = 250 ml or 1 cup.*

• *To make self-raising flour, add 5 ml gluten-free baking powder for every 250 ml of flour called for.*

Gluten-free flours

Almond flour

Buckwheat flour

Chickpea flour

Coconut flour

Cornflour (Maizena, maize flour)

Flax seed flour

Macadamia nut flour

Potato flour/starch

Quinoa flour

Rice flour (brown and white rice flour)

Sorghum flour

Sunflower seed flour

Tapioca flour/starch

Teff flour

Notes • *Where a recipe calls for 'gluten-free flour', you can use any one of these flours, or a combination of them.*

Gluten-free grains

Amaranth	Polenta
Buckwheat	Quinoa
Corn	Rice
Maize meal (mealiepap)	Sago
Millet	Sorghum
Oats *	Teff

* Unless the packaging states that oats are gluten-free, they may have been processed in a factory that also makes wheat-based products, so cross-contamination can occur.

Gluten-containing flours and grains

Bulgur wheat

Couscous

Pearl barley

Rye flour

Semolina

Spelt flour

Wheat flour (cake wheat flour, wholewheat flour, bread flour, self-raising flour)

Breakfast

Ricotta hotcakes

Serve these warm with crispy bacon and maple syrup.

250 g ricotta cheese
180 ml milk
2 eggs, separated

250 ml gluten-free flour mix
   (see page 8)
5 ml baking powder

30 ml castor sugar
3 ml salt
oil for frying

1. Combine the ricotta, milk and egg yolks in a bowl and mix well.
2. Sift the gluten-free flour, baking powder, castor sugar and salt. Add to the ricotta and mix to combine.
3. Beat the egg whites until stiff and fold into the mixture.
4. Heat a little oil in a nonstick frying pan. Drop spoonfuls of mixture into the pan and cook until bubbles appear on the surface, then turn them over and cook on the other side until golden in colour.

Makes 10–12

Almond crumpets

Serve with crispy bacon and sliced avocado, topped with a spoonful of sour cream or cream cheese.

100 g ground almonds
60 ml psyllium husks
60 ml coconut flour
30 ml ground flax seeds (linseeds)
30 ml xylitol
10 ml baking powder

60 g butter, melted
125 ml cream
2 eggs
250 ml full-cream milk
coconut oil for frying

1. Combine the ground almonds, psyllium husks, coconut flour, ground flax seeds, xylitol and baking powder in a bowl.
2. Combine the melted butter, cream, eggs and milk and stir into the dry ingredients. Set aside for 15 minutes to thicken up.
3. Melt a little coconut oil in a nonstick frying pan over a medium heat. Add a spoonful of the mixture, spreading it out slightly, and cook until firm enough to turn over and cook on the other side.

Makes 10–12

Note *These crumpets are quite fragile to cook, so make sure your heat is not too high or they will burn before they have cooked long enough to set and turn.*

Honey oat muffins

250 ml gluten-free rolled oats

500 ml gluten-free flour (see page 8)

125 ml buckwheat flour or coconut flour

125 ml tapioca starch

5 ml baking powder

3 ml bicarbonate of soda

3 ml salt

250 ml coconut milk

125 ml apple sauce

3 extra large eggs

125 ml oil

125 ml honey

1. Combine the oats, flours, tapioca starch, baking powder, bicarbonate of soda and salt in a bowl and mix well.
2. Add the coconut milk, apple sauce, eggs, oil and honey and mix gently (just until the dry ingredients are moistened).
3. Line a 12-cup muffin pan with paper liners and divide the mixture between them.
4. Bake in a preheated oven at 180°C for 20–30 minutes, or until a skewer inserted into the centre of the muffins comes out clean. Remove from the oven and place on a rack to cool.

Makes 12

Banana oat crumpets

These are delicious served with a drizzle of honey or maple syrup.

250 ml gluten-free rolled oats

5 ml baking powder

15 g ground almonds

10 ml castor sugar or xylitol

3 ml salt

1 banana, mashed

150 ml almond milk

coconut oil for frying

1. Process the oats in a food processor or blender until finely ground.
2. Transfer to a bowl and add the baking powder, ground almonds, castor sugar and salt.
3. Mix in the banana and almond milk. Let the batter stand for 10 minutes.
4. Heat a little coconut oil in a nonstick frying pan. Drop spoonfuls of the mixture into the pan and cook until bubbles appear on the surface of the crumpets, then turn them over and cook on the other side.

Makes 10–12

Lemon poppy seed muffins

100 g ground almonds
250 ml gluten-free flour (see page 8)
5 ml baking powder
2 ml salt

60 ml poppy seeds
30 ml coconut oil, melted
2 eggs
125 ml honey

125 ml coconut milk or almond milk
5 ml vanilla extract
zest of 2 lemons

1. Combine the ground almonds, gluten-free flour, baking powder, salt and poppy seeds in a bowl.
2. In a jug, whisk together the melted coconut oil, eggs, honey, coconut milk, vanilla extract and lemon zest.
3. Make a well in the centre of the dry ingredients and pour in the liquid ingredients. Mix well until just combined.
4. Line a 12-cup muffin pan with paper liners and divide the mixture between them.
5. Bake in a preheated oven at 180°C for 15–20 minutes, or until a skewer inserted into the centre of the muffins comes out clean. Remove from the oven and place on a rack to cool.

Makes 12

Berry oat bars

250 g fresh or frozen blackberries or raspberries

45 ml chia seeds

30–40 ml xylitol or castor sugar

5 ml vanilla essence

125 ml gluten-free oats

125 ml brown rice flour

125 ml xylitol

80 ml tapioca flour/starch

50 g ground almonds

5 ml ground cinnamon

3 ml bicarbonate of soda

3 ml xanthan gum

2 ml salt

125 g butter, cubed

1. Mash the berries with a potato masher. Place in a saucepan with the chia seeds and 30–40 ml xylitol and stir to combine. Set aside for 20 minutes, then heat the mixture and simmer for 3–5 minutes until slightly thickened. Remove from the heat and stir in the vanilla essence. Set aside until completely cool.
2. Combine all the remaining dry ingredients in a bowl and mix well. Rub in the butter until well blended.
3. Line a 20 x 30 cm baking tray with baking paper. Press three-quarters of the oats mixture into the tray.
4. Spread over the cool berry mixture, then sprinkle the remaining crumble on top.
5. Bake in a preheated oven at 180°C for 50–60 minutes, until golden brown. Remove from the oven and leave in the tray to cool completely before cutting into squares. Store in an airtight container.

Makes 15

Breakfast bars

100 g whole blanched almonds, lightly toasted

100 g walnuts or pecan nuts, lightly toasted

150 g mixed dried berries

500 ml mixed seeds, including some chia seeds

125 ml desiccated coconut

60 ml psyllium husks

3 ml salt

5 ml vanilla extract

2 eggs

45 ml honey

1. Roughly chop the toasted nuts and place in a bowl with the dried berries, seeds, coconut, psyllium husks and salt. Mix well to combine.
2. Beat the vanilla extract, eggs and honey in a small bowl. Add to the seed and nut mixture and stir until well combined.
3. Grease and line a 25 x 25 cm square baking tray with baking paper. Scoop the mixture into the tray and press down firmly with the back of a spoon.
4. Bake in a preheated oven at 180°C for 20 minutes until golden brown. Remove from the oven and cool in the tray before cutting into squares. Store in an airtight container.

Makes 12

Quinoa porridge

10 ml coconut oil

250 ml quinoa

500 ml almond milk

60 ml maple syrup

5 ml vanilla extract

pinch of ground cinnamon

60 ml coconut milk

30 ml honey

For serving

125 ml desiccated coconut, toasted

25 g slivered almonds, lightly toasted

250 ml fresh berries

mint leaves, for garnish (optional)

1. In a saucepan, heat the coconut oil over a medium heat.
2. Add the quinoa and toast for 2–3 minutes until it has a slightly nutty aroma.
3. Add the almond milk and bring to a simmer. Once the almond milk is simmering, add the maple syrup, vanilla extract and cinnamon.
4. Cover, and reduce the heat to low. Cook for 18–20 minutes, until the quinoa is tender and all the liquid has been absorbed.
5. Divide the quinoa between 2 bowls. Drizzle with the coconut milk and honey and serve immediately, topped with toasted coconut and almonds, and your choice of fresh berries.

Serves 2

Almond butter bars

250 ml almond butter

125 ml honey

2 eggs

2 ml bicarbonate of soda

80 ml desiccated coconut

60 g almonds, toasted and chopped

1. In the bowl of an electric mixer, blend together the almond butter, honey, eggs and bicarbonate of soda until creamy.
2. Fold in the coconut and toasted almonds.
3. Grease and line an 18 x 20 cm rectangular baking tray, allowing the baking paper to overhang. Pour the batter into the prepared tray.
4. Bake in a preheated oven at 180°C for 15–20 minutes until just set and barely starting to brown. Remove from the oven and cool in the tray before cutting into bars. Store in an airtight container.

Makes 10–12

Breakfast rösti

Serve these topped with a poached egg. If preferred, you can substitute sautéed mushrooms for the bacon.

2 medium potatoes, peeled and grated
1 small onion, peeled and grated
125 ml gluten-free flour (see page 8)
5 ml baking powder

salt and ground black pepper
2 eggs, beaten
250 g chopped bacon, fried and
    drained on paper towel

100 g Cheddar cheese, grated
60 ml chopped fresh parsley
oil for frying
poached eggs, for serving

1. Combine the grated potato and onion in a bowl.
2. Sprinkle over the flour, baking powder and seasoning to taste and mix through.
3. Add the eggs and mix well.
4. Fold through the bacon, cheese and parsley.
5. Heat a little oil in a frying pan and drop spoonfuls of the mixture into the pan. Flatten with the back of a spoon (so they are not too thick).
6. Fry over a medium heat until golden brown, then turn and cook until golden on the other side. Drain on paper towel. Serve topped with a poached egg.

Makes 14–15

Quinoa granola

500 ml rolled oats

125 ml quinoa

100 ml coconut flakes

80 g flaked almonds

50 g pecan nuts, roughly chopped

125 ml pumpkin seeds

60 ml sesame seeds

200 ml maple syrup

5 ml vanilla extract

5 ml ground cinnamon

150 g dried cranberries

1. Combine the oats, quinoa, coconut, nuts and seeds in a large bowl. Mix well.
2. Combine the maple syrup and vanilla extract in a jug. Add to the oat mixture and stir until evenly distributed.
3. Sprinkle over the cinnamon and blend well.
4. Spread the granola evenly on a large baking sheet lined with baking paper and bake in a preheated oven at 120°C for 50–60 minutes, stirring after about 25 minutes. Remove and set aside to cool. Toss in the cranberries. Store in a sealed container for up to 4 weeks.

Makes 14–16 servings

Home-made muesli

This is delicious served with Greek yoghurt and honey.

500 g gluten-free rolled oats

125 ml sunflower seeds

125 ml flax seeds (linseeds)

125 ml sesame seeds

125 ml pumpkin seeds

60 ml chia seeds

100 g almonds, roughly chopped

100 g hazelnuts, roughly chopped

125 ml xylitol

15 ml ground cinnamon

250 ml water

125 ml coconut oil

375 ml coconut flakes

150 g raisins or sultanas

150 g dried blueberries

150 g dried cranberries

50 g dried goji berries

1. Combine the oats, seeds, nuts, xylitol and cinnamon in a large bowl. Mix well.
2. Add the water and stir through. Set aside for 30 minutes.
3. Add the coconut oil and mix well.
4. Spread the mixture in a single layer on 1 large or 2 medium baking trays that have been lined with baking paper.
5. Bake in a preheated oven at 170°C for 30–40 minutes.
6. Add the coconut flakes and return to the oven until the flakes are lightly browned.
7. Remove from the oven and toss through the raisins and dried berries. When cool, store in an airtight container for up to 1 month.

Makes 14–16 servings

Blueberry brunch cake

125 g butter, softened
180 ml castor sugar
10 ml finely grated lemon rind
2 eggs

5 ml vanilla extract
500 ml gluten-free flour mix (see page 8)
5 ml xanthan gum
10 ml baking powder

160 ml buttermilk
150 g fresh or frozen blueberries
30 ml brown sugar

1. Cream the butter and castor sugar in a large bowl until light and creamy. Fold in the lemon rind.
2. Add the eggs, one at a time, beating after each addition. Beat in the vanilla extract.
3. Sift together the flour mix, xanthan gum and baking powder.
4. Add to the creamed mixture alternately with the buttermilk.
5. Gently fold in the blueberries.
6. Spoon the mixture into a greased and lined 20 x 20 cm square cake pan. Sprinkle over the brown sugar.
7. Bake in a preheated oven at 180ºC for 30–40 minutes, or until a skewer inserted into the centre comes out clean. Remove from the oven and leave to cool in the pan. Cut into squares to serve.

Makes ± 25 squares

Waffles

Serve these with syrup and whipped cream for a decadent weekend treat.

500 ml gluten-free flour mix (see page 8)
7 ml baking powder
3 ml bicarbonate of soda

5 ml xanthan gum
30 ml castor sugar
3 eggs, separated

250 ml buttermilk
300 ml water
30 ml sunflower oil

1. Combine the flour mix, baking powder, bicarbonate of soda, xanthan gum and castor sugar in a bowl.
2. Add the egg yolks, buttermilk, water and sunflower oil, and mix to a thick batter.
3. Beat the egg whites until stiff and fold into the batter.
4. Spray a waffle iron with nonstick cooking spray and heat it up. Place spoonfuls of the batter into the waffle iron and cook until the waffles are golden and crisp. Remove from the waffle iron and place on a rack in a warm oven to prevent them from going soft while you cook the rest of the waffles.

Makes 8–10

Lunch

Quinoa crustless quiche

250 ml water

125 ml quinoa

10 ml olive oil

1 onion, peeled and diced

1 garlic clove, crushed

60 ml gluten-free flour (see page 8)

4 eggs

60 ml milk

200 g feta cheese, cubed

100 g mature Cheddar cheese, grated

80 ml grated Parmesan cheese

4 Roma tomatoes, seeded and diced

100 g black olives, pitted and halved

60 ml fresh basil, shredded

salt and ground black pepper to taste

1. To cook the quinoa, bring the water and quinoa to the boil in a small saucepan. Reduce to a simmer, cover and cook for 15 minutes. Turn off the heat and leave the covered saucepan on the stove for an additional 5 minutes, then remove the lid and fluff the quinoa with a fork. Set aside.
2. Heat the oil in a frying pan and sauté the onion and garlic until tender.
3. Whisk together the flour, eggs and milk in a large bowl.
4. Add the quinoa, sautéed onion and the rest of the ingredients to the egg mixture and mix well.
5. Pour into an ovenproof dish greased with nonstick cooking spray and bake in a preheated oven at 180°C for 30–40 minutes until golden brown and set. Remove from the oven and leave to cool for 10 minutes. Slice and serve hot or cold.

Serves 4–6

Spinach and tuna roulade

The tuna can be replaced with canned salmon, smoked salmon ribbons or smoked trout.

Spinach roulade

300 g fresh spinach, washed

4 eggs, separated

250 ml grated Parmesan cheese

50 g Cheddar cheese, grated

Tuna filling

2 cans (170 g each) tuna chunks in brine, drained and flaked

60 ml cream cheese

60 ml sour cream

30 ml chopped piquanté peppers

60 ml chopped fresh parsley

10 ml lemon juice

salt and ground black pepper to taste

1. Cook the spinach in a little water until wilted, about 5 minutes. Drain thoroughly and squeeze out any moisture. Chop finely, place in a large bowl and set aside to cool.
2. When cool, mix in the egg yolks and stir in the cheeses. Season to taste with salt and ground black pepper.
3. In a separate bowl, whisk the egg whites until stiff. Gently fold into the spinach mixture.
4. Pour the spinach mixture into a greased and lined 24 x 35 cm Swiss roll tray, spreading it into the corners.
5. Bake in a preheated oven at 180°C for 10–12 minutes, until set and light golden brown. Turn out the roulade onto a large sheet of greaseproof or baking paper. Peel away the lining and leave to cool.
6. Combine all the filling ingredients in a bowl, mixing well. Spread evenly over the cooled roulade, then roll up like a Swiss roll, using the greaseproof paper to guide you. Place on a serving platter with the join underneath. Chill until ready to serve.

Serves 6

Ratatouille crumble

50 ml olive oil

2 red onions, peeled and cut into wedges

15 ml chopped garlic

2 brinjals, cubed

3–4 large baby marrows, chopped into
   2-cm pieces

1 each red, yellow and green pepper,
   seeded and diced

1 can (400 g) chopped tomatoes

10 ml sugar, or to taste

salt and ground black pepper, to taste

100 g feta or goat's cheese, crumbled

Crumble

500 ml gluten-free breadcrumbs

50 g butter, melted

30 ml pesto

45 ml chopped fresh parsley

45 ml chopped fresh basil

1. Heat the oil in a frying pan and gently fry the onions and garlic until soft.
2. Add the brinjals, baby marrows, peppers and canned tomatoes. Bring to a simmer and cook for 20–30 minutes, until the vegetables are tender. Remove from the heat, add the sugar and season with salt and pepper
3. Gently mix through the cheese, then spoon the filling into a greased ovenproof baking dish.
4. Combine all the crumble ingredients in a bowl, mixing well. Sprinkle on top of the ratatouille filling.
5. Bake in a preheated oven at 180°C for 15–20 minutes until the crumble is golden brown and crispy. Serve hot.

Serves 4

Caramelized onion, bacon and blue cheese crustless quiche

15 ml olive oil

2 onions, peeled, halved and sliced

30 ml honey

250 g bacon, cooked and diced

125 g blue cheese, crumbled

4 eggs, slightly beaten

125 ml milk

125 ml potato flour

100 g mozzarella cheese, grated

60 ml grated Parmesan cheese

salt and ground black pepper

1. Heat the oil in a frying pan, add the onions and brown over low-to-medium heat, stirring frequently.
2. Add the honey and continue cooking over a low heat for 10–15 minutes until the onions are caramelized. Remove from the heat, and arrange the cooked onions on the bottom of a greased ovenproof baking dish or pie dish.
3. Scatter over the bacon and half the blue cheese.
4. Combine the eggs, milk and potato flour and whisk well. Whisk in the cheeses and season to taste.
5. Pour the egg mixture over the onions and bacon. Dot with the remaining blue cheese.
6. Bake in a preheated oven at 180°C for 20–30 minutes until set (it should not be wobbly).

Serves 6

Quinoa tabbouleh salad

Traditional tabbouleh is made with bulgur (cracked wheat), which is not gluten-free. This version, made with quinoa, is a good substitute.

250 ml quinoa
375 ml water
pinch of salt
½ English cucumber, seeded and sliced
125 g baby tomatoes, halved

1 red pepper, seeded and diced
1 avocado, diced
80 ml chopped fresh parsley
80 ml chopped fresh mint, plus extra,
    for garnish (optional)

Dressing
60 ml lemon juice
45 ml olive oil
5 ml chopped garlic
salt and ground black pepper to taste

1. Place the quinoa in a sieve and rinse well under running water. Put the water and salt in a saucepan and add the quinoa. Bring to the boil, then cover and simmer for about 20 minutes until the quinoa is cooked and soft. Drain through a sieve and spread the quinoa on a baking tray to cool.
2. In a serving bowl, combine the quinoa with the cucumber, tomatoes, red pepper, avocado and herbs. Toss well to combine.
3. Combine all the ingredients for the dressing and mix well. Pour the dressing over the salad and serve.

Serves 4–6

Quinoa vegeburgers

30 ml olive oil
1 large onion, peeled and finely chopped
10 ml chopped garlic
5 ml curry powder
5 ml ground cumin

3 ml turmeric
2 carrots, peeled and grated
4 small baby marrows, grated
salt and ground black pepper
500 ml cooked quinoa (see Note, below)

250 ml fresh gluten-free breadcrumbs
125 ml grated Parmesan cheese
1 egg
oil for frying

1. Heat the oil in a frying pann and fry the onion and garlic over a medium heat until soft. Add the spices and cook for 1 minute.
2. Add the carrots and baby marrows and fry for 5 minutes. Remove from the heat. Season well.
3. Add the cooked quinoa, breadcrumbs, Parmesan cheese and egg and mix well.
4. Shape the mixture into patties. Place on a board or baking sheet and refrigerate for at least 1 hour.
5. Heat a little oil in a frying pan over a medium-high heat and fry the patties until golden brown on each side. Drain on paper towel. These can be served either hot or cold.

Makes 8–10

Note *Quinoa swells when cooked (like rice), so 250 ml raw quinoa will yield 500 ml when cooked.*

Quinoa quiche with kale and feta

Quinoa is used to make the base of the quiche. It needs to be baked until it is crisp or it may become soggy when the filling is added.

Base

400 ml water

180 ml quinoa

5 ml salt

250 ml finely grated Parmesan cheese

1 egg, lightly beaten

Filling

45 ml oil

1 onion, peeled and chopped

10 ml chopped garlic

500 ml cleaned chopped kale or spinach

salt and ground black pepper

60 ml chopped fresh mint

180 g feta cheese, crumbled

50 g Cheddar cheese, grated

250 ml cream

4 eggs

Base

1. To cook the quinoa, place the water, quinoa and salt in a small saucepan. Bring to the boil, then reduce to a simmer, cover and cook for 15–20 minutes. Turn off the heat, but leave the covered saucepan on the stove for an additional 5 minutes, then remove the lid and fluff the quinoa with a fork.

2. Remove the saucepan from the heat and stir the Parmesan cheese and egg into the quinoa, mixing well.

3. Press the mixture firmly into the base and sides of a greased 22-cm pie plate or a loose-bottomed quiche pan.

4. Bake in a preheated oven at 180°C for 20–25 minutes until lightly brown and crisp. Remove from the oven and set aside to cool.

Filling

1. Heat the oil in a frying pan and fry the onion and garlic until soft.

2. Add the kale and stir-fry for about 10 minutes until tender. Remove from the heat and season well.

3. Add the mint and feta cheese and stir through.

4. Sprinkle the grated Cheddar cheese over the quiche base. Top with the kale mixture.

5. Beat together the cream and eggs. Season well, then pour over the kale mixture.

6. Bake in a preheated oven at 180°C for 25–30 minutes, until the surface is golden and the centre is firm.

7. Remove the quiche from the oven and serve warm or cold. (If you are using a loose-bottomed pan, leave the quiche to stand for 10 minutes before removing it from the pan.)

Serves 4–6

Chickpea burgers

30 ml oil, plus extra for frying
1 onion, peeled and chopped
2 garlic cloves, crushed
10 ml curry powder
2 small baby marrows, grated
1 can (400 g) chickpeas, drained
   and rinsed

2 slices gluten-free bread,
   dried and crumbled
1 egg
30 ml chopped fresh coriander
salt and ground black pepper to taste
gluten-free flour for dusting

For serving
4 gluten-free seed bread rolls (see below)
thinly sliced red onion
sliced tomato
fresh rocket
double cream (Greek) yoghurt

1. Heat the oil in a frying pan and gently fry the onion and garlic until soft. Add the curry powder and cook for 1 minute.
2. Add the baby marrows and cook for 2–3 minutes. Transfer to a bowl and set aside to cool.
3. Put the chickpeas in a food processor or blender and process until finely chopped. Add the chickpeas to the baby marrows, along with the breadcrumbs, egg, coriander and seasoning. Mix well.
4. Shape the mixture into 4 patties. Dust with a little gluten-free flour and refrigerate for a few hours.
5. Heat a little oil in a frying pan and cook the patties until golden brown on both sides.
6. Serve on gluten-free rolls, with sliced onion and tomato, rocket and some Greek yoghurt.

Makes 4

Seed bread rolls

These rolls won't stay fresh for longer than a day, so turn any leftover rolls into crumbs and keep them in the freezer for recipes that require gluten-free breadcrumbs.

470 g Health Connection Wholefoods
   gluten-free brown bread flour
125 ml mixed seeds
30 ml castor sugar
10 ml salt

2 x 10 g sachets instant yeast
5 ml xanthan gum
300 ml warm milk
100 ml olive oil
2 eggs

5 ml apple cider vinegar
   or white grape vinegar
beaten egg for glazing
sesame seeds for sprinkling

1. Mix the flour, seeds, castor sugar, salt, yeast and xanthan gum in the bowl of an electric mixer fitted with a paddle attachment.
2. Combine the milk, olive oil, eggs and vinegar and add to the flour mixture. Mix well for about 5 minutes to form a thick batter.
3. Spoon the batter into muffin cups that have been greased with nonstick cooking spray or a little margarine. Cover with a clean cloth and leave to rise for 1 hour.
4. Brush the tops of the rolls with beaten egg and sprinkle with sesame seeds.
5. Bake in a preheated oven at 180°C for 20 minutes, or until a skewer inserted into the rolls comes out clean. Remove from the oven and place on a rack to cool.

Makes 12–14

Roasted vegetable and quinoa salad

5–6 baby marrows, thickly sliced

2 red onions, peeled, halved, and cut
   into thin wedges

1 brinjal, cut into 2-cm pieces

1 red pepper, seeded and diced

60 ml olive oil

salt and ground black pepper

250 g cherry tomatoes

1 garlic clove, crushed

10 ml ground cumin

250 ml quinoa

500 ml water

1 can (400 g) chickpeas, drained
   and rinsed

50 g black olives, pitted

120 g feta cheese, cubed

Dressing

60 ml olive oil

30 ml lemon juice

salt and ground black pepper to taste

fresh basil leaves for garnishing

1. Place the baby marrows, onions, brinjal and red pepper on an oven tray. Drizzle with half the olive oil and season to taste. Roast in a preheated oven at 180°C for 15 minutes.

2. Add the cherry tomatoes to the tray and roast for a further 10 minutes, or until all the vegetables are tender.

3. Meanwhile, heat the remaining olive oil in a saucepan over a medium heat. Add the garlic and cumin and stir-fry for 30 seconds until aromatic.

4. Add the quinoa and water. Bring to the boil, then reduce the heat to low. Cover and simmer for 15–20 minutes, or until the quinoa is tender and the water has been absorbed. Remove from the heat and leave to cool slightly in the saucepan. Fluff the quinoa with a fork and place in a serving bowl.

5. Add the roasted vegetables and the remaining salad ingredients to the quinoa.

6. For the dressing, whisk the ingredients together in a jug or small bowl. Pour over the salad and toss gently to combine. Garnish with fresh basil.

Serves 6

Cauliflower 'couscous' salad

Couscous is not gluten-free, so this salad uses cauliflower instead. It is refreshingly different and extremely healthy.

1 cauliflower, washed and broken
    into florets
1 red chilli, seeded and finely chopped
125 ml fresh mint, chopped
125 ml fresh coriander, chopped
1 red onion, peeled and finely chopped
zest of 1 lemon

1 bunch spring onions, thinly sliced
salt and ground black pepper to taste
50 g flaked almonds, toasted
125 ml pomegranate rubies or
    dried cranberries

Lemon vinaigrette
50 ml lemon-flavoured olive oil
15 ml sherry vinegar or red wine vinegar
juice and zest of 1 lemon
125 ml olive oil
15 ml honey
salt and ground black pepper

1. Put the cauliflower florets into a food processor and pulse until they are crumbly and look like couscous.
2. Transfer to a bowl and add the chilli, mint, coriander, red onion, lemon zest and spring onions. Mix to combine.
3. For the vinaigrette, place the lemon-flavoured olive oil, vinegar, lemon juice and zest into a bowl and whisk to an emulsion. Slowly add the olive oil, whisking continually until combined. Mix in the honey and season with salt and pepper.
4. To serve, season the cauliflower to taste with salt and pepper and dress with the lemon vinaigrette. Scatter over the flaked almonds and pomegranate rubies.

Serves 6–8

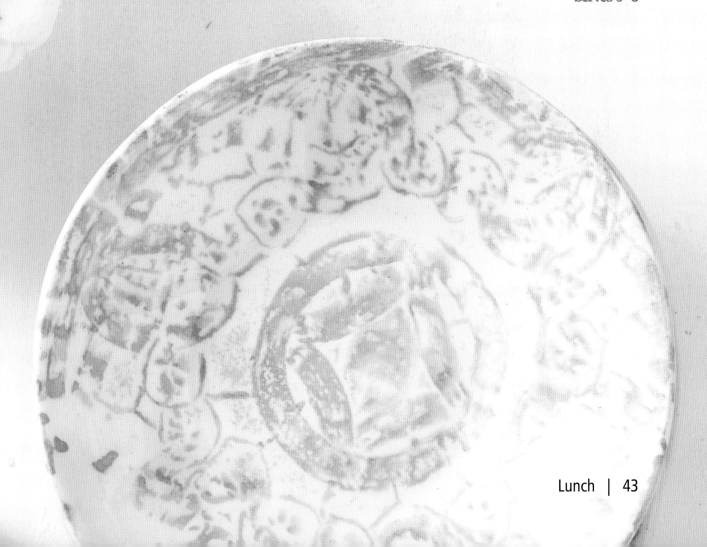

Tuna and potato patties

These are delicious served hot or cold.

30 ml olive oil, plus extra for frying

1 onion, peeled and chopped

2 potatoes, peeled, cooked and mashed

1 can (170 g) tuna chunks in brine,
   drained and flaked

4 small gherkins, finely chopped

grated zest and juice of 1 lemon

60 ml chopped fresh parsley

salt and ground black pepper to taste

1 egg, beaten

500 ml fresh gluten-free breadcrumbs

tzatziki, for serving

1. Heat the olive oil in a small frying pan and fry the onion until soft and golden.

2. Place the mashed potato, tuna, gherkins, lemon zest and juice, parsley and seasoning in a bowl and add the fried onion.

3. Add the egg and mix well.

4. Shape the mixture into patties and coat each with breadcrumbs. Place on a baking tray and refrigerate for at least 1 hour.

5. Heat a little oil in a frying pan. Fry the patties over a medium heat until golden brown on both sides. Drain on paper towel.
    Serve with tzatziki.

Makes 8–10 'hamburger'-size patties

Low-carb buns

Make these buns in shallow muffin pans, or collect tuna cans and bake individual buns in them. You can also use this recipe to make a single loaf of bread.

250 ml mixed seeds

250 ml sunflower seeds

60 g (150 ml) ground almonds

60 ml psyllium husks

30 ml xylitol

20 ml gluten-free baking powder

5 ml salt

250 ml buttermilk

6 eggs, beaten

1. Grind the mixed seeds and sunflower seeds in a coffee grinder or NutriBullet® until you have a fine, flour-like mixture. Place in a bowl with the ground almonds, psyllium husks, xylitol, baking powder and salt and stir to combine.

2. Add the buttermilk and eggs and mix well. Leave to stand for 15 minutes to thicken up.

3. Grease the cups of a wide (8 cm), shallow muffin pan (Yorkshire pudding pans are ideal), or use 8 tuna cans. To make a loaf, use an 18 x 9 cm loaf pan lined with baking paper and greased. Spoon the mixture into each cup or into the loaf pan.

4. Bake in a preheated oven at 180°C (15–20 minutes for buns; 30–40 minutes for a loaf, or until a skewer inserted into the centre comes out clean).

Makes 8–10

Seed crackers

These are great with dips and spreads, on a cheese board, or topped with your favourite cold meats or some mashed avocado. They will keep for up to a month in an airtight container.

250 ml flax seeds (linseeds)
250 ml sesame seeds
250 ml sunflower seeds

50 ml chia seeds
50 ml psyllium husks
45 ml pumpkin seeds

5 ml salt
30–40 ml mixed dried herbs
500 ml cold water

1. Combine all the ingredients in a large bowl and leave to soak for 15–20 minutes until the water is absorbed. Mix well.
2. Line two 30 x 40 cm baking trays with baking paper and spray with nonstick cooking spray. Divide the mixture and spread evenly over the prepared trays. Score the dough into squares with a knife.
3. Bake in a preheated oven at 180°C for 15–20 minutes. Flip the crackers over, switch off the oven and leave the crackers to cool in the oven until crisp.

Makes 40–50

Cornflour seed loaf

80 ml flax seeds (linseeds)
475 ml warm water
10 g sachet instant yeast
100 ml plain yoghurt

4 x 250 ml (500 g) cornflour (Maizena)
125 ml psyllium husks
5 ml castor sugar
5 ml salt

45 ml olive oil
beaten egg for glazing

1. Spread the flax seeds on a baking tray and bake in a preheated oven at 180°C for 10–12 minutes, or until they darken slightly. Set aside to cool.
2. Place the water and yeast in a bowl. Stir in the yoghurt and toasted flax seeds.
3. In a large mixing bowl, stir together the cornflour, psyllium husks, castor sugar and salt.
4. Pour in the yeast mixture and the olive oil, and mix to make a smooth thin batter. Leave to stand for 5–10 minutes until it becomes a sticky dough.
5. Once the mixture is firm enough, knead it on the work surface for a few minutes. Place the dough in a bowl, cover with cling wrap and leave to rise for 30 minutes.
6. Line a baking tray with nonstick baking paper. Shape the dough into a fat sausage shape and place on the tray. Brush with beaten egg, cover with a clean cloth and leave to rise for another 30 minutes.
7. Slash the top of the loaf with a sharp knife. Bake in a preheated oven at 200°C for 40–50 minutes, or until a skewer inserted into centre of the loaf comes out clean.

Makes 1 large free-form loaf

Cheesy polenta corn bread

625 ml polenta

250 ml gluten-free self-raising flour
(see page 8)

200 g Cheddar cheese, grated

5 ml baking powder

3 ml bicarbonate of soda

5 ml xanthan gum

15 ml castor sugar

5 ml salt

1 can (400 g) corn kernels, drained

60 ml chopped fresh chives

500 ml buttermilk

125 g butter, melted

3 eggs, lightly whisked

1. Combine the polenta, flour, Cheddar cheese, baking powder, bicarbonate of soda, xanthan gum, sugar and salt in a large bowl.
2. Stir in the corn and chives until well combined.
3. Combine the buttermilk, melted butter and eggs and pour into the dry ingredients. Mix until just combined.
4. Pour the mixture into a greased and lined loaf pan (20 x 10 cm) and smooth the surface.
5. Bake in a preheated oven at 180°C for 40–45 minutes, or until a skewer inserted into the centre comes out clean. Serve warm with butter.

Makes 1 large loaf or 4 mini loaves

Health bread

250 ml pumpkin seeds

250 ml brown rice flour

250 ml ground almonds

50 ml psyllium husks

125 ml sunflower seeds

125 ml extra pumpkin seeds

60 ml sesame seeds

30 ml chia seeds

30 ml mixed dried herbs

5 ml salt

400 ml water

60 ml coconut oil

2 eggs, beaten

1. Grind the 250 ml pumpkin seeds to a fine, flour-like meal in a coffee grinder or NutriBullet®.
2. Place the ground pumpkin seeds in a bowl with the brown rice flour, ground almonds and psyllium husks and mix well.
3. Mix in the sunflower seeds, whole pumpkin seeds, sesame seeds, chia seeds, mixed herbs and salt.
4. Combine the water, coconut oil and eggs and add to the dry ingredients. Mix well. Set the mixture aside for 30 minutes to become firm.
5. Spoon the mixture into a standard loaf pan (20 x 10 cm) greased with nonstick cooking spray.
6. Bake in a preheated oven at 180°C for 1 hour, or until a skewer inserted into the centre of the loaf comes out clean. Remove from the oven and cool in the pan for 10 minutes before turning out onto a cooling rack.

Makes 1 standard loaf

Onion bhajis with spicy red sauce

160 ml chickpea flour

60 ml rice flour

10 ml gluten-free baking powder

5 ml chilli powder

5 ml ground cumin

3 ml turmeric

5 ml salt

2 extra large eggs, beaten

100 ml water

250 ml fresh coriander, chopped

3–4 onions, peeled, halved and
    thinly sliced

oil for frying

Spicy red sauce

1 can (400 g) chopped tomatoes

1 red pepper, seeded and diced

2 red chillies, seeded and finely chopped

2 garlic cloves, finely chopped

45 ml brown sugar

30 ml brown vinegar

1. Sift all the dry ingredients into a bowl.

2. Combine the eggs and water and slowly add to the dry ingredients, whisking to make a smooth batter.

3. Add the coriander and onions and stir through.

4. Pour a shallow layer of oil into a frying pan and heat. Fry spoonfuls of the mixture in batches, adding more oil if necessary.
    Drain on paper towel and serve hot with the spicy red sauce.

Spicy red sauce

1. Combine all the ingredients in a saucepan and simmer until reduced and thickened.
    If you prefer a smooth sauce, place the cooked sauce in a food processor or blender and process until smooth.

Serves 6—8

Garden vegetable and feta crustless quiche

4 baby marrows, sliced

½ yellow, red and green peppers, seeded and diced

1 small broccoli, cut into florets

1 cooked potato, peeled and diced

250 g button mushrooms, halved

30 ml olive oil

3 sprigs fresh thyme, leaves stripped

salt and ground black pepper to taste

180 g feta cheese

4 eggs

125 ml milk

125 ml gluten-free flour (see page 8)

5 ml gluten-free baking powder

2 ml salt

10 ml gluten-free prepared mustard

100 g Cheddar cheese, grated

2 tomatoes, sliced

fresh rosemary or other herbs, for garnishing (optional)

1. Place the prepared vegetables in a roasting dish and drizzle with the olive oil. Scatter over the thyme leaves and season to taste with salt and pepper.

2. Roast in a preheated oven at 180°C for 15–20 minutes until the vegetables are tender. Remove and set aside to cool.

3. Roughly crumble the feta cheese into the cooled vegetables.

4. In a large bowl, whisk together the eggs, milk, gluten-free flour, baking powder, salt, mustard and Cheddar cheese. Add the roasted vegetables and mix gently to combine.

5. Pour the mixture into a large, greased ovenproof dish. Top with the sliced tomato and bake in a preheated oven at 180°C for 20–30 minutes, or until set. Garnish with fresh herbs and serve warm.

Serves 6

Cheesy ham and veggie slice

This can be served hot or cold, making it perfect for a brunch or for packing into lunch boxes.
For a vegetarian version, substitute the ham for finely sliced button mushrooms.

15 ml olive oil

1 large onion, peeled and chopped

125 g good-quality ham, finely chopped

400 g baby marrows, coarsley grated

2 carrots, peeled and coarsely grated

80 g Cheddar cheese, grated

80 ml gluten-free flour mix (see page 8)

6 eggs, beaten

80 ml milk

salt and ground black pepper to taste

fresh rosemary or other herbs,
    for garnishing (optional)

1. Heat the oil in a frying pan and fry the onion until soft. Remove from the pan and set aside to cool.
2. Combine the cooled onions, ham, baby marrows and carrots in a bowl.
3. Add the Cheddar cheese and flour mix and stir to combine.
4. Mix the eggs and milk together and add to the ham and vegetable mixture. Season well.
5. Pour the mixture into a 18 x 28 cm baking tray lined with nonstick baking paper.
6. Bake in a preheated oven at 180°C for 25–30 minutes, or until golden brown and set. Leave to cool in the tray, then remove and cut into squares. Garnish with fresh herbs before serving.

Makes 8 squares

Spinach and Parmesan soufflé

30 g butter

30 ml gluten-free flour mix (see page 8)

200 ml milk

200 g packet baby spinach, washed,
    drained and chopped

10 ml gluten-free mustard prepared
    (Dijon-style), optional

100 ml grated Parmesan cheese

50 g white Cheddar cheese, grated

3 eggs, separated

salt and ground black pepper to taste

pinch of cayenne pepper, or to taste

softened butter for greasing

50 ml dried gluten-free breadcrumbs

1. Melt the butter in a saucepan over a medium heat. Add the flour mix and stir until the mixture is smooth. Reduce the heat and cook, stirring, for 1 minute.
2. Gradually add the milk, stirring until the mixture is smooth. Bring to the boil and cook until the mixture thickens.
3. Add the spinach and mustard, if using, and cook until the spinach is wilted.
4. Remove from the heat and stir in the cheeses. Stir in the egg yolks and season to taste. Transfer the mixture to a bowl.
5. Brush the base and sides of six 200-ml ovenproof ramekins with the softened butter and lightly coat with breadcrumbs. Shake out any excess crumbs.
6. Preheat the oven to 200°C. In a separate bowl, whisk the egg whites until stiff, but not dry. Using a large metal spoon, gently fold the egg whites into the warm spinach mixture until just combined.
7. Spoon the mixture into the prepared ramekins and place the ramekins on a baking tray. Bake for 15–20 minutes until the soufflés are puffed up and golden. Serve immediately.

Makes 6 individual soufflés

Dinner

Spicy quinoa and sweet potato soup

1 kg sweet potatoes, peeled and chopped
15 ml oil
1 onion, peeled and chopped
30 ml grated fresh ginger
2 red chillies, seeded and chopped

5 ml ground cumin
125 ml quinoa
500 ml gluten-free vegetable stock
2 stalks lemongrass, bruised with a
    rolling pin

1 can (400 g) coconut milk
125 ml chopped fresh coriander
fresh coriander leaves, for garnishing
red chillies, for garnishing

1. Put the sweet potatoes into a saucepan with cold water. Bring to the boil, cover and simmer for 10–15 minutes until soft. Drain and set aside.
2. Heat the oil in a saucepan and lightly cook the onion, ginger, chillies and cumin.
3. Add the quinoa, vegetable stock and lemongrass and simmer, covered, until the quinoa is tender (15–20 minutes). Remove the lemongrass and discard.
4. Remove the saucepan from the heat. Add the sweet potatoes, coconut milk and chopped coriander to the saucepan and blend with a hand-held blender until smooth.
5. Return the saucepan to the stove and stir over medium heat until the soup is heated through. Garnish with coriander leaves and sliced red chilli (optional) and serve.

Serves 4–6

Quinoa crumbed fish

This recipe is ideal for using up leftover quinoa. If you don't have precooked quinoa, prepare it according to the package instructions.

250 ml cold cooked quinoa

125 ml grated Parmesan cheese

salt and ground black pepper to taste

60 ml chopped fresh parsley

2 large eggs, beaten

250 ml gluten-free flour (see page 8)

4 fresh fish fillets

sunflower oil for frying

lemon wedges for serving

1. Combine the cooked quinoa, Parmesan cheese, seasoning and parsley and mix well. Place in a shallow bowl.
2. Put the beaten eggs in another shallow bowl and the gluten-free flour in a third shallow bowl.
3. Dip the fish fillets first into the gluten-free flour, then into the beaten egg and finally into the quinoa mixture (turning them each time to make sure they are coated on both sides).
4. Heat a little oil in a frying pan. Fry the fish (in batches if necessary) until cooked and golden and crisp on both sides. Drain on paper towel. Serve immediately with lemon wedges.

Serves 4

Battered fish

Batter for fish is traditionally made with beer, but as beer isn't gluten-free we've replaced it with soda water.

125 ml gluten-free self-raising flour

125 ml cornflour (Maizena)

5 ml salt

1 extra large egg, separated

200 ml soda water

sunflower oil for frying

4 fresh fish fillets

125 ml gluten-free flour for dredging

lemon wedges for serving

1. Combine the gluten-free self-raising flour and cornflour in a bowl. Add the salt.
2. Add the egg yolk and soda water to the flour and mix to form a smooth batter.
3. In a separate bowl, beat the egg white until stiff. Gently fold into the batter.
4. Pour enough oil into a saucepan or deep frying pan to cover the fish fillets. Heat the oil until bubbles start to rise.
5. Place the gluten-free flour in a shallow dish. Dip the fish fillets, one by one, into the gluten-free flour (turning them to make sure they are coated on both sides).
6. Dip the coated fillets, one by one, into the batter mixture, making sure they are well covered.
7. Carefully lower the battered fillets into the hot oil and fry (in batches if necessary) until cooked and golden and crisp on both sides. Drain on paper towel. Serve immediately with lemon wedges.

Serves 4

Salmon pasta bake

250 g gluten-free pasta shapes

80 g butter

1 onion, peeled and chopped

60 ml chickpea or other gluten-free flour

180 ml gluten-free chicken stock

500 ml milk

5 ml salt

ground black pepper to taste

250 g button mushrooms, sliced

150 g frozen peas

2 cans (213 g each) pink salmon, drained and flaked

zest and juice of 1 lemon

100 g Cheddar cheese, grated

45 ml grated Parmesan cheese

1. Cook the pasta according to package instructions. Drain and set aside.
2. Melt the butter in a saucepan and fry the onion until soft.
3. Stir in the gluten-free flour and cook for a minute.
4. Gradually add the chicken stock and milk, stirring constantly, until the mixture boils and thickens. Season to taste.
5. Add the cooked pasta, mushrooms, peas, salmon, lemon zest and juice and stir through.
6. Mix in the Cheddar cheese and spoon into an ovenproof dish. Sprinkle over the Parmesan cheese.
7. Bake in a preheated oven at 180°C for 20–25 minutes until golden brown.

Serves 6

Mac and three cheeses

Traditional mac-'n-cheese gets a boost with a trio of cheeses; make it mild for family meals or use a mature Cheddar when you want to tantalize your tastebuds.

200 g quinoa pasta or other gluten-free short pasta

50 g butter

60 ml gluten-free flour (see page 8)

375 ml milk

5 ml gluten-free Dijon mustard, optional

salt and ground black pepper to taste

80 g each Cheddar, Parmesan and mozzarella cheese, grated (you need 240–250 g in total)

60 ml chopped fresh parsley

125 ml dried gluten-free breadcrumbs

60 ml grated Parmesan cheese

1. Cook the pasta according to the package instructions. Drain and set aside.
2. Melt the butter in a large saucepan and add the gluten-free flour. Cook for 1 minute.
3. Gradually add the milk, stirring constantly over a medium heat until the mixture boils and thickens. Remove from the heat and stir in the mustard (if using) and seasoning to taste.
4. Stir in the three cheeses and the parsley.
5. Add the cooked, drained pasta to the sauce, mixing well. Spoon the sauce into an ovenproof dish.
6. Combine the breadcrumbs and grated Parmesan cheese and scatter over the pasta.
7. Bake in a preheated oven at 180°C for 20–25 minutes until golden and bubbling. Serve immediately.

Serves 4

Vegetable lasagne

Make this ahead, ready to cook just before dinner. Or bake and freeze, either as a family meal or in individual portions, for convenience. Home-made gluten-free pasta dough is fragile and can't take too much shaping, but it is ideal for making lasagne sheets, or cut into thin strips for spaghetti or linguine.

Gluten-free pasta dough

500 ml gluten-free flour (see page 8)

10 ml xanthan gum

5 ml salt

20 ml olive oil

2–3 eggs

rice flour for dusting

Roasted vegetable sauce

1 large brinjal, diced

3 mixed peppers, seeded and diced

4–6 large baby marrows, cut into
    1-cm-thick slices

2 red onions, peeled and cut into wedges

45 ml olive oil

salt and ground black pepper

2 cans (400 g each) chopped tomatoes

150 ml white wine

10 ml chopped garlic

45 ml tomato paste

45 ml chopped fresh basil

White sauce

50 g butter

80 ml chickpea or other gluten-free flour

750 ml milk at room temperature

50 g Cheddar cheese, grated

salt and ground black pepper

To assemble

100 g feta cheese, crumbled

grated Parmesan cheese

Pasta dough

1. Place the gluten-free flour, xanthan gum and salt in a food processor. Pulse to break up any lumps.

2. With the motor running, add the olive oil and 2 eggs. Lightly whisk the third egg and add just enough to form a soft ball.

3. As soon as the dough comes together, remove and knead on a lightly floured surface for 5 minutes until smooth. Wrap the dough in cling wrap and leave to rest for 30 minutes at room temperature.

4. Divide the dough into 8 equal portions (cover with cling wrap to prevent them drying out). Flatten 1 portion and dust with rice flour, if needed. Set a pasta machine on the thickest setting. Feed the dough through the machine while turning the handle. Fold each short end of dough into the centre to form a smaller rectangle and roll out again. Repeat this process twice more until the dough comes out smooth.

5. Close the gap between the rollers of the pasta machine by 1 setting. Continue rolling and folding the dough until you have a long strip about 1.5 mm thick. Cut the pasta into sheets to fit your dish (see assembly instructions). Repeat the rolling process with the remaining portions of dough. If you are not using the pasta right away, place the cut sheets on a tray covered with a clean dish cloth and leave to dry, turning frequently. Once the pasta is completely dry, it can be stored in an airtight container.

Vegetable sauce

1. Combine the brinjal, peppers, baby marrows and red onions in a roasting pan. Drizzle with the olive oil and season to taste with salt and ground black pepper.

2. Roast in a preheated oven at 180°C for 30 minutes, or until the vegetables are soft. Remove and set aside.

3. In the meantime, put the tomatoes into a saucepan. Add the wine, garlic and tomato paste. Bring to the boil, lower the heat and simmer for 15–20 minutes. Add the basil and season to taste with salt and pepper. Remove from the heat.

4. Add the roasted vegetables to the tomato sauce and mix well.

White sauce

1. Melt the butter in a saucepan. Add the chickpea flour and cook for 2 minutes.
2. Add the milk, whisking all the time, and bring to the boil.
3. Lower the heat and add the Cheddar cheese. Cook for 1 minute, stirring continuously until the cheese has melted. Season to taste and remove from the heat.

To assemble

1. Spoon about one-third of the white sauce into the base of a 20 x 30-cm ovenproof casserole dish. Arrange a layer of lasagne sheets over the sauce, cutting them to fit if necessary.
2. Spoon over half the vegetable sauce, crumble over half the feta cheese and pour over one-third of the white sauce. Position another layer of lasagne sheets and repeat the other ingredients, ending with white sauce. (You should have 2 layers.)
3. Top with a good sprinkling of grated Parmesan cheese.
4. Bake in a preheated oven at 180°C for 25–35 minutes until the top is golden brown and the lasagne is heated through.

Serves 6–8

Gluten-free pizza

Everyone loves pizza! With this gluten-free option, the whole family will be able to enjoy home-made pizza.

Pizza base

750 ml gluten-free flour (see page 8)

50 g ground almonds

60 ml psyllium husks

10 ml baking powder

10 g sachet instant yeast

10 ml salt

30 ml castor sugar

60 ml olive oil

400–500 ml warm water

Topping

250 ml gluten-free tomato pasta sauce

300 g mozzarella cheese, grated

10 ml mixed dried herbs

baby tomatoes, halved

sliced prosciutto

fresh basil or rocket leaves or other fresh
   herbs for garnishing

Pizza base

1. Combine the gluten-free flour, ground almonds, psyllium husks, baking powder, yeast, salt and castor sugar in the bowl of a mixer or food processor. Using the K-beater or paddle attachment, mix until blended.

2. With the machine running, add the oil and enough warm water to form a dough that is soft but not too sticky. Mix for at least 5 minutes. Cover the bowl and set aside to rise in a warm place for 1 hour.

3. Knead the dough gently, then divide it into 4 portions. On a lightly floured surface, roll each portion into a disc about 20 cm in diameter. Place on a baking tray lined with nonstick baking paper. Cover and leave to rise for another 30 minutes.

4. Bake in a preheated oven at 200°C for 10–15 minutes to set the base. Remove from the oven and cool slightly before adding the topping.

Topping

1. Spread each base with some of the tomato pasta sauce, leaving the edges clear.

2. Scatter over the mozzarella cheese, mixed dried herbs and fresh basil leaves, if using.

3. Return to the oven and bake at 200°C for 8–12 minutes until the cheese is bubbling and the base is golden brown.

4. Remove and top with halved baby tomatoes, prosciutto and fresh basil or rocket leaves before serving.

Makes 4 medium (± 20 cm) pizzas

Note *To save time, make the bases in advance and freeze them. Bake the bases for 10 minutes, as described above, then leave them to cool before wrapping each one in cling wrap and freezing for up to 4 weeks. To use, remove the base from the freezer, defrost, add your toppings and bake at 200°C for 10–15 minutes.*

Cauliflower and almond flatbread with roasted baby marrows and mint pesto

Flatbreads

350 g cauliflower, broken into florets

150 g ground almonds

45 ml psyllium husks

180 ml grated Parmesan cheese

2 eggs

5 ml salt

coconut flour for rolling

Mint pesto

20–30 g fresh mint leaves, plus extra
  leaves for garnishing

15–20 g fresh Italian parsley

5 ml chopped garlic

25 g ground almonds

125 ml grated Parmesan cheese

1 wedge preserved lemon, rind only,
  chopped, optional

lemon juice to taste

salt and ground black pepper to taste

125 ml olive oil

Roasted baby marrow topping

2–3 large baby marrows, trimmed and
  thinly sliced lengthways

olive oil for cooking

125 g ricotta or feta cheese, crumbled

Flatbreads

1. Place the cauliflower florets in the bowl of a food processor and pulse until finely chopped.

2. Add the remaining ingredients, except the coconut flour, and process for 2–3 minutes until well blended. Set aside
   for 20 minutes.

3. Divide the mixture into 5 portions. Dust a work surface well with coconut flour. Roll each portion into a disc about 20 cm
   in diameter and place on a baking tray lined with a silicone mat or nonstick baking paper.

4. Bake the flatbreads in a preheated oven at 200°C for 10–15 minutes until golden brown.

Pesto

1. Place the herbs, garlic and ground almonds in a food processor and pulse until the herbs are chopped.

2. Add the Parmesan cheese, preserved lemon rind (if using), lemon juice and seasoning and pulse until blended.

3. With the machine running, slowly add the olive oil.

4. Check the seasoning and adjust to taste.

Topping

1. Brush the baby marrow slices with olive oil. Place in a single layer in a preheated griddle pan and cook until the flesh starts
   to char. Drain on paper towel.

2. Spread the warm flatbreads with mint pesto. Sprinkle with ricotta or feta cheese and top with baby marrow slices. Garnish
   with fresh mint leaves or other fresh herbs of your choice and serve immediately.

Makes 5 flatbreads

Polenta pizza with bacon, onions, mushrooms and mozzarella

Polenta pizza base

625 ml water

250 ml milk

5 ml salt

250 ml polenta

30 ml olive oil

salt and ground black pepper
   for sprinkling

Tomato base

125 g sun-dried tomatoes

45 ml basil pesto

50 ml water

salt and ground black pepper to taste

Toppings

125 g streaky bacon, fried and chopped

200 g exotic mushrooms, sliced and fried

1 red onion, cut into half-moons

2–3 small mozzarella balls, torn into
   bite-sized chunks

5 ml dried origanum

cherry tomatoes, halved

1 avocado, peeled and sliced

rocket leaves

Pizza base

1. Grease a 38 x 26 cm baking tray with nonstick cooking spray or brush with olive oil.

2. Combine the water, milk and salt in a saucepan. Bring to the boil, then reduce to a simmer.

3. Add the polenta in a steady stream, whisking constantly to prevent lumps. Cover with the lid and cook over a low heat for 5–10 minutes, stirring occasionally. If the mixture becomes too thick, whisk in a bit more boiling water. Stir in the olive oil.

4. Spoon the polenta into the prepared tray, working quickly so that the polenta does not stiffen. With wet hands, press it to a thickness of about 5 mm all over. Sprinkle with salt and pepper.

5. Cover the tray with cling wrap and refrigerate for about 1 hour until firm. (For convenience, make the base ahead and leave it in the fridge for up to a day before cooking.) Bake the polenta in a preheated oven at 200°C for 20–30 minutes, or until it begins to brown and crisp on the edges.

Tomato base

1. Combine all the ingredients in a food processor or blender and blend until smooth. Set aside.

Toppings

1. Spread a layer of tomato base over the polenta. Top with the bacon, mushrooms, red onion, torn mozzarella and origanum.

2. Bake in a preheated oven at 200°C for 10–15 minutes until the cheese begins to melt and the bacon and vegetables are warmed through.

3. Remove from the oven and top with cherry tomatoes, avocado and rocket leaves. Cut into squares and serve hot.

Makes 4–6 squares

Quinoa vegetable bake

Serve squares or slices of this 'crustless quiche' as a vegetarian main course.

250 ml quinoa

500 ml water

2 ml salt

30 ml butter

1 onion, peeled and finely chopped

350 g broccoli, cut into florets

250 g button mushrooms, sliced

150 g exotic mushrooms, sliced

1 red pepper, seeded and chopped

125 g basil pesto

2 eggs

100 g Cheddar cheese, grated

250 g ricotta cheese
   or plain cottage cheese

250 g sour cream

salt and ground black pepper

extra grated Cheddar cheese,
   for sprinkling

1. Place the quinoa, water and salt in a small saucepan. Bring to the boil, then reduce to a simmer, cover and cook for 15–20 minutes. Turn off the heat and leave in the covered saucepan for a further 10 minutes. Fluff with a fork and set aside.

2. Melt the butter in a large saucepan. Add the onion and cook for about 5 minutes.

3. Add the broccoli, all the mushrooms and the red pepper and cook until just softened, about 5 minutes. Add the pesto and stir through. Remove from the heat and stir in the quinoa.

4. Beat the eggs in a medium bowl and stir in the cheeses and sour cream. Mix well. Season with salt and black pepper and fold into the vegetable-quinoa mixture.

5. Spray a 20 x 25 cm ovenproof dish with nonstick cooking spray. Spread the mixture into the prepared dish and top with the extra grated Cheddar cheese.

6. Bake in a preheated oven at 180°C for 30–35 minutes until set.

Serves 6

Seed-crusted chicken fillets with creamy avocado pesto

100 g ground almonds

375 ml mixed seeds

250 ml finely grated Parmesan cheese

5 ml salt

2 ml ground black pepper

2 ml cayenne pepper (or chilli flakes
or smoked paprika)

60 ml finely chopped fresh parsley

60 ml finely chopped fresh chives

2 eggs

400 g mini skinless chicken breast fillets
(or slice larger fillets into strips)

60 ml coconut oil

60 g butter

Creamy avocado pesto

1 avocado, peeled and diced

250 ml fresh basil leaves

50 g blanched almonds

30 ml olive oil

5 ml crushed garlic

3 ml salt

juice and finely grated zest of 1 lemon

1. Combine the ground almonds, mixed seeds, Parmesan cheese, salt, black pepper, cayenne pepper, parsley and chives in a bowl.

2. Whisk the eggs in a shallow dish.

3. Dip the chicken fillets first into the egg and then into the seed mixture. Place on a greased baking tray and refrigerate for at least 30 minutes.

4. Heat the coconut oil and butter together in a frying pan until hot. Fry the chicken, in batches, until golden on each side. Serve warm with avocado pesto. (These can also be served cold.)

Pesto

1. Place all the ingredients in a blender or food processor and process until smooth. Store in an airtight container and refrigerate for up to 2 days.

Serves 4

Bolognese with rice noodles

30 ml olive oil

1 onion, peeled and chopped

2 garlic cloves, crushed

2 stalks celery, chopped

1 large carrot, peeled and coarsely grated

500 g beef mince

1 can (400 g) chopped Italian tomatoes

30 ml tomato paste

250 ml gluten-free beef stock, or water

5 ml dried basil

5 ml dried origanum

5 ml sugar

salt and ground black pepper to taste

250 g medium rice noodles, prepared
   according to package instructions

finely grated Parmesan-style cheese
   for serving

1. Heat the oil in a saucepan and gently fry the onion, garlic, celery and carrot until soft.

2. Add the mince and brown well, breaking up any lumps as you go.

3. Add the tomatoes, tomato paste, stock, herbs, sugar and seasoning and simmer, uncovered, for 20–30 minutes until the sauce thickens.

4. Drain the prepared noodles, add to the meat sauce and toss to combine. Sprinkle with Parmesan cheese before serving.

Serves 4

Sun-dried tomato and olive millet burgers

Millet, the key ingredient in these burgers, is a healthy, gluten-free grain that is gaining popularity.

250 ml millet

750 ml water or vegetable stock

30 ml olive oil, plus extra for frying

1 red onion, peeled and finely chopped

5 ml chopped garlic

4–5 sun-dried tomatoes in oil,
   drained and chopped

100 g green olives, drained, pitted
   and chopped

45 ml capers, chopped

80 ml grated Parmesan cheese

60 ml chopped fresh basil

salt and ground black pepper

1. Combine the millet and water in a saucepan and simmer until the millet is cooked and all the liquid is absorbed. Remove from the heat and set aside, covered, for 10 minutes.

2. Heat the 30 ml olive oil and fry the onion and garlic until soft. Add to the millet.

3. Stir in the sun-dried tomatoes, olives, capers, Parmesan cheese, basil and seasoning to taste (the mixture will be quite sticky).

4. Shape the mixture into patties and place on a baking tray or plate. Refrigerate for 1 hour or more.

5. Heat some olive oil in a frying pan and fry the burgers over a medium heat for 3–4 minutes on each side. Serve as desired.

Makes 6–8

Note *Millet, an ancient cereal, features in the traditional cuisine of China, India and Africa. A gluten-free whole grain, it is found in products such as seeded breads, roti (flatbreads) and seed-based energy bars.*

Pork larb in lettuce cups

Larb is a Thai salad that includes minced meat. If you don't eat pork, use chicken mince instead.
Baby cos or baby gem lettuce works best for this dish.

30 ml oil

1 onion, peeled and chopped

15 ml chopped garlic

500 g pork mince

15–30 ml fish sauce

30 ml fresh lime juice

10–15 ml sriracha sauce

15 ml sweet chilli sauce

15 ml brown sugar

45 ml chopped fresh mint

45 ml chopped fresh basil

45 ml chopped fresh coriander

lettuce leaves, for serving

double cream yoghurt, for serving

1. Heat the oil in a frying pan and fry the onion and garlic over a medium-high heat until the onion is soft but not brown.
2. Add the mince and fry until nicely browned, breaking up the lumps with a wooden spoon.
3. Add the fish sauce, lime juice, sriracha sauce, sweet chilli sauce and brown sugar and mix to combine.
4. Remove from the heat and add the chopped herbs. Spoon into cup-shaped lettuce leaves, top with yoghurt.

Serves 4

Asian-style chicken with rice noodles

125 g medium rice noodles

30 ml peanut oil

4 chicken breast fillets, sliced into 'stir-fry' strips

2 carrots, peeled and julienned

1 red onion, peeled and thinly sliced

250 g button mushrooms, sliced

10 ml chopped garlic

15 ml chopped ginger

60 ml tamari (wheat-free soy sauce)

15–30 ml fish sauce

10 ml sesame oil

15 ml lime juice

30 ml sweet chilli sauce

60 ml chopped fresh coriander, for serving

1. Put the rice noodles in a bowl and cover with hot water. Set aside for 20–30 minutes, or until soft.
2. Heat the peanut oil in a wok or frying pan and fry the chicken strips until just cooked. Remove and set aside.
3. Heat a little more oil in the same pan and add the carrots, onion, mushrooms, garlic and ginger. Stir-fry until just tender.
4. Combine the tamari, fish sauce, sesame oil, lime juice and sweet chilli sauce in a bowl and mix well.
5. Add the sauce to the vegetables and stir through. Return the chicken to the pan and heat through.
6. Drain the noodles and add to the chicken and vegetables. Mix until well combined. Serve sprinkled with chopped coriander.

Serves 4–6

Roast beef with gravy and Yorkshire pudding

The classic English roast dinner tends to be reserved for special occasions, so it's good to know you can still enjoy it with trimmings like Yorkshire pudding, pumpkin fritters (see opposite) and roasted cauliflower (see page 81).

Roast beef and gravy

1.8–2 kg beef roast

30 ml olive oil

15 ml gluten-free wholegrain mustard

salt and ground black pepper to taste

1 carrot, peeled and roughly chopped

1 onion, peeled and roughly chopped

1 stalk celery, roughly chopped

375 ml beef stock

15 ml cornflour (Maizena) mixed with a
    little cold water to make a paste

15 ml butter

1.   Place the meat in an oven roasting pan.

2.   Combine the oil, mustard and seasoning in a small bowl. Rub the mixture all over the surface fat layer of the meat.

3.   Add the carrot, onion, celery and stock to the roasting pan.

4.   Roast in a preheated oven at 180°C for 20 minutes per 500 g. Remove the meat from the pan, cover loosely with foil and leave to rest for 10 minutes before slicing.

5.   While the meat is resting, prepare the gravy. Strain the pan juices into a small saucepan and bring to the boil.

6.   Stir in the cornflour paste. Cook, stirring, until the mixture boils and thickens. Adjust the seasoning to taste and stir in the butter to give the gravy a glossy appearance.

Serves 6

Yorkshire pudding

180 ml gluten-free flour mix (see page 8)

60 ml cornflour (Maizena)

5 ml salt

3 ml xanthan gum

3 eggs, beaten

375 ml milk

30 g butter, melted

sunflower oil for baking

1.   Combine the gluten-free flour mix, cornflour, salt and xanthan gum in a bowl and mix well.

2.   Combine the eggs, milk and melted butter and add to the dry ingredients, mixing to form a batter.

3.   Place about 10 ml sunflower oil in each cup of a 12-cup muffin pan. Place the muffin pan in a preheated oven at 200°C for 15 minutes, until the oil is smoking hot. Carefully remove the pan from the oven and very quickly divide the batter between the cups, filling each one about three-quarters full.

4.   Return the pan to the oven and bake for 25–30 minutes, or until the Yorkshire puddings are puffed and golden. Remove from the oven and serve immediately with the roast beef and gravy.

Makes 12 (serve 2 per portion)

Pumpkin fritters

These are traditionally served warm as a vegetable side dish.

375 ml cooked mashed pumpkin
  (± 500 g raw pumpkin)

250 ml gluten-free flour (see page 8)

5 ml salt

10 ml baking powder

30 ml castor sugar

2 extra large eggs, beaten

sunflower oil for shallow frying

cinnamon sugar for dredging
  (see below)

1. Combine the pumpkin, gluten-free flour, salt, baking powder and castor sugar in a bowl and mix thoroughly.
2. Add the eggs and mix to form a thick batter.
3. Heat a little oil in a frying pan and fry spoonfuls of the batter, a few at a time, until bubbles appear on the surface and the underside is golden brown. Flip the fritters over and cook on the other side. Remove and drain on paper towel before dredging with cinnamon sugar.

Cinnamon sugar

1. Combine 125 ml granulated or castor sugar with 10 ml ground cinnamon.

Makes 14–16

Roasted cauliflower with cashew basil cream sauce

This cashew cream sauce is very versatile; serve it over cooked gluten-free pasta or raw veggie noodles. It's also delicious as a salad dressing. Serve this as a vegetarian meal or as an accompaniment to meat, chicken or fish.

Roasted cauliflower

1 medium whole cauliflower, leaves
    removed and stem trimmed

60 ml olive oil

30 ml lemon juice

15 ml ground cumin

salt and ground black pepper to taste

Cashew basil cream sauce

125 g raw, unsalted cashew nuts

1 can (400 g) coconut milk

45 ml lemon juice

5 ml chopped garlic

125 ml fresh basil leaves

salt and ground black pepper to taste

Cauliflower

1. Line a baking tray with heavyweight foil. Place the cauliflower on the tray.

2. Combine the olive oil, lemon juice, cumin, and salt and pepper to taste in a bowl and rub the mixture all over the cauliflower.

3. Roast in a preheated oven at 160°C for 1 hour until tender. Remove from the oven. Transfer the roasted cauliflower to a serving dish and pour over the cashew basil cream sauce.

Sauce

1. Soak the cashew nuts in cold water for 1 hour, to soften.

2. Drain the cashew nuts and place in a blender or food processor with the rest of the ingredients. Blend continuously for 5 minutes until smooth and thick. Check the seasoning and adjust to taste.

Serves 4

Dessert

Low-carb lemon cheesecake

Nut crust

65 g ground almonds

65 g pecan nuts, ground

125 ml desiccated coconut

15 ml xylitol or castor sugar

100 ml coconut oil, melted

Filling

2 tubs (250 g each) thick cream cheese

80 ml xylitol or castor sugar

80 ml lemon juice

10 ml lemon zest

3 eggs

5 ml vanilla extract

250 ml cream, whipped

fresh strawberries for decorating

icing sugar, for dusting (optional)

Crust

1. Combine the nuts, coconut and xylitol in a bowl.

2. Add the coconut oil and mix well to combine.

3. Press the mixture into the base of a 20-cm springform cake pan, levelling it with your fingertips.

4. Wrap the base and sides of the pan in a double layer of foil and place in the freezer while you prepare the filling.

Filling

1. Beat the cream cheese and xylitol in a bowl until smooth and creamy.

2. Gradually beat in the lemon juice and zest.

3. Add the eggs and vanilla extract and beat until combined.

4. Pour the mixture onto the chilled base. Put the cake pan into a deep-sided oven pan and pour in boiling water to come halfway up the sides of the cake pan.

5. Bake in a preheated oven at 150°C for 30–40 minutes, or until the filling is set but still has a slight wobble in the centre. Switch off the oven and open the door slightly. Leave the cheesecake to cool in the oven for 1 hour, then take the cake pan out of the water and refrigerate until well chilled.

6. Remove the foil from around the pan. Slide a flat-bladed knife around the edge of the pan, then release the spring and remove the pan. Slide the knife under the crust to loosen it, then slide the cheesecake onto a serving plate. Refrigerate until required. Just before serving, top with whipped cream and halved or whole strawberries. Dust with icing sugar, if preferred.

Note *To make a biscuit base, replace the nuts with 200 g crushed gluten-free biscuits mixed with 100 g melted butter.*

Serves 8–10

No-bake milk tart

Although the pastry crust requires baking, it can be made in advance. To make this a real 'no-bake' dessert, use a nut crust instead (see pages 85 and 108).

Crust

1 quantity gluten-free shortcrust pastry
   (see page 148)

Filling

1 can (385 g) condensed milk
500 ml full-cream milk
75 ml cornflour (Maizena)
30 ml custard powder

2 eggs, beaten
5 ml vanilla essence
30 g butter
gluten-free ground cinnamon
   for sprinkling

Crust

1. Roll out the chilled pastry and line a 25-cm quiche pan or pie plate.
2. Prick the base. Line with nonstick baking paper and fill with dried beans.
3. Bake blind in a preheated oven at 180°C for 10–15 minutes, until pale golden brown.
4. Remove the baking paper and beans and return to the oven at 180°C for a further 5 minutes, to finish baking the crust. Remove from the oven and leave to cool before adding the filling.

Filling

1. Put the condensed milk and 250 ml of the milk into a saucepan and heat to just boiling.
2. Combine the cornflour and custard powder in a mixing bowl. Add the remaining 250 ml milk and mix until smooth.
3. Mix in the eggs.
4. Add some of the hot milk mixture to the cornflour mixture and stir to combine. Pour the cornflour mixture into the saucepan and stir over a medium heat until it comes to the boil and thickens.
5. Remove from the heat and stir in the vanilla essence and butter.
6. Pour the mixture into the cooled pastry shell and sprinkle over some cinnamon. Refrigerate until set.

Serves 12–14

Flourless chocolate cake

This cake has the added advantage of being low-carb as well as gluten-free.

150 g dark chocolate, broken up

150 g butter at room temperature, cubed

5 eggs

125 ml xylitol or castor sugar

5 ml vanilla extract

150 g ground almonds

mixed fresh berries for serving

whipped cream for serving

1. Combine the chocolate and butter in a glass bowl. Microwave on low (50% power) for 2–3 minutes until the chocolate is melted and the mixture is smooth. Stir only at the end. Set aside to cool.
2. Using an electric mixer, beat the eggs and xylitol in a large bowl until thick and creamy. Beat in the vanilla extract.
3. Beat the cooled chocolate mixture into the egg mixture. Fold in the ground almonds.
4. Spoon the mixture into a lined and greased 20-cm cake pan.
5. Bake in a preheated oven at 160°C for 30–40 minutes, or until a skewer inserted into the centre of the cake comes out clean. Remove from the oven and leave to cool in the pan (the cake will sink slightly in the middle as it cools).
6. Remove the cake from the pan. Pile with mixed berries and serve with whipped cream on the side.

Serves 8–10

Malva pudding

2 extra large eggs

250 ml castor sugar

15 ml smooth apricot jam

310 ml gluten-free flour mix (see page 8)

5 ml bicarbonate of soda

5 ml xanthan gum

pinch of salt

30 g butter

125 ml milk

5 ml vinegar

Sauce

250 ml cream

125 ml white sugar

100 g butter

100 ml brandy, optional

whipped cream for serving

1. Beat the eggs and castor sugar in a large bowl until light and fluffy. Mix in the apricot jam.
2. Sift together the dry ingredients.
3. Melt the butter and combine with the milk and vinegar.
4. Alternately add the milk mixture and the dry ingredients to the egg mixture, mixing well after each addition.
5. Pour the mixture into a greased 20 x 25 cm ovenproof dish. Bake in a preheated oven at 180°C for 30–40 minutes.
6. Remove from the oven, poke holes with a skewer and immediately pour over the sauce.

Sauce

1. Put the cream, white sugar and butter into a saucepan and bring to the boil.
2. Remove from the heat and add the brandy (if using). Pour the hot sauce over the pudding and leave it to soak in. Serve warm with whipped cream.

Serves 6

Sticky toffee pudding

250 g dried pitted dates, chopped
500 ml boiling water
10 ml bicarbonate of soda
10 ml vanilla extract
100 g butter
375 ml white sugar
2 eggs

750 ml gluten-free flour mix (see page 8)
10 ml gluten-free baking powder

Toffee sauce
250 ml cream
125 ml brown sugar
125 ml white sugar

125 ml golden syrup
100 g butter
5 ml vanilla extract

1. Put the dates into a bowl and pour over the boiling water. Stir in the bicarbonate of soda and vanilla extract and leave to cool.
2. In a separate bowl, cream the butter and white sugar well.
3. Add the eggs, one at a time, mixing well before each addition.
4. Sift the dry ingredients and add to the creamed mixture alternately with the cooled date mixture. Mix well.
5. Pour the mixture into a deep 20 x 30 cm ovenproof baking dish that has been greased with butter.
6. Bake in a preheated oven at 180°C for 30–40 minutes until cooked. Remove from the oven and prick all over with a skewer. Pour over the toffee sauce and leave for up to 10 minutes so that the sauce can soak into the pudding. If not serving immediately, leave to cool and reheat before serving.

Sauce
1. Put all the ingredients into a saucepan and heat until the sugars dissolve. Bring to the boil and cook for 5 minutes. Pour the hot sauce over the pudding as soon as it comes out of the oven.

Serves 6–8

Pancakes with mascarpone, mango and raspberry purée

Pancakes

250 ml gluten-free flour mix (see page 8)

2 eggs, beaten

250 ml coconut milk

150 ml water

15 ml coconut oil

Filling

250 g fresh raspberries

15–30 ml xylitol or castor sugar

250 g mascarpone cheese

1–2 mangoes, peeled and diced

icing sugar for dusting, optional

Pancakes

1. Put the gluten-free flour mix into a mixing bowl.

2. Combine the eggs, coconut milk, water and coconut oil in a jug and mix well.

3. Add to the dry ingredients and mix until smooth; it should be the consistency of pouring cream.

4. Preheat a small (20-cm) nonstick frying pan. Pour in just enough batter to coat the base of the pan and cook the pancake for 1 minute on each side.

5. Continue until all the batter is used. Stack the cooked pancakes on a plate, with a sheet of greaseproof paper or wax paper between each one. (You can reheat them in the microwave, if necessary.)

Filling

1. Purée the raspberries (reserving some for garnishing) and pass the purée through a sieve to remove the pips.

2. Sweeten to taste with xylitol.

3. Spread each cooked pancake with some mascarpone cheese. Top with diced mango and drizzle over some raspberry purée .

4. Roll up the pancakes. Top with fresh raspberries and dust with icing sugar, if desired. Serve immediately.

Makes 8—10

Apple and blueberry crumble

1 can (400 g) pie apples,
   roughly chopped
250 g fresh blueberries
125 ml castor sugar
15 ml lemon juice
5 ml vanilla extract

Crumble
125 ml gluten-free flour (see page 8)
45 ml brown sugar
50 g butter
60 ml gluten-free rolled oats
25 g flaked almonds

45 ml shredded coconut
5 ml gluten-free ground cinnamon
   (optional)

1. Combine the apples, blueberries, castor sugar, lemon juice and vanilla extract in a bowl and mix well, but gently.
2. Divide the mixture between 4–6 ovenproof ramekins. Place the ramekins on a baking tray. (Instead of individual ramekins, you can use an ovenproof baking dish.)
3. Top generously with crumble and bake in a preheated oven at 180°C for 15–20 minutes until the crumble is golden. (For a single dish, bake for 25–40 minutes.)

Crumble

1. Place the gluten-free flour, brown sugar and butter in a food processor and pulse until the mixture resembles coarse breadcrumbs. (You can also rub the butter in using your fingertips, if you prefer.)
2. Stir in the oats, flaked almonds, coconut and ground cinnamon (if using).

Makes 4–6

Lemon passionfruit pudding

4 eggs, separated

325 ml milk

160 ml lemon juice

15 ml very finely grated lemon zest

250 ml gluten-free flour (see page 8)

5 ml gluten-free baking powder

pinch of salt

250 ml castor sugar

150 ml passionfruit pulp

melted butter for greasing

icing sugar for dusting

whipped cream for serving

1. Whisk the egg yolks, milk, lemon juice and lemon zest in a bowl.
2. Sift over the gluten-free flour, baking powder, salt and 180 ml of the castor sugar. Whisk until smooth and combined.
3. Stir in the passionfruit pulp.
4. Place the egg whites in a clean, dry bowl. Using an electric mixer, beat them until soft peaks form.
5. Beat in the remaining castor sugar until thick and glossy.
6. Gently fold the egg-white mixture into the lemon mixture.
7. Pour the mixture into 6 individual ramekins (or a 1.2-litre ovenproof baking dish) greased with melted butter and place in a roasting pan. Add enough boiling water to the pan to come halfway up the sides of the ramekins (or the baking dish).
8. Bake in a preheated oven at 170°C for 20–25 minutes (30–35 minutes for a baking dish), or until golden and set. Dust with icing sugar and serve with whipped cream.

Serves 6

Lemon tart

Crust

1 quantity gluten-free shortcrust pastry
   (see page 148)

Lemon filling

3 eggs

250 ml castor sugar

180 ml cream

125 ml lemon juice

10 ml very finely grated lemon zest

Crust

1. Roll out the chilled pastry and line the base and sides of a 20-cm loose-bottomed quiche pan.
2. Cover the pastry with baking paper and weigh it down with baking beans.
3. Bake blind in a preheated oven at 180°C for 10 minutes. Remove the paper and beans and return the crust to the oven to bake for another 10 minutes until the pastry is pale golden. Remove and set aside to cool.

Filling

1. In a bowl, beat the eggs and castor sugar well.
2. Mix in the cream, lemon juice and lemon zest.
3. Carefully pour the filling into the cooled pastry case.
4. Bake in a preheated oven at 160°C for 15–20 minutes until just set. Remove and set aside to cool. Chill well before serving.

Serves 6—8

Low-carb brownies

50 g dark chocolate, roughly chopped

125 ml coconut oil

125 ml cocoa powder

100 g ground almonds

30 ml coconut flour

4 eggs

180 ml xylitol or castor sugar

45 ml almond butter

5 ml vanilla extract

5 ml gluten-free baking powder

2 ml salt

60 ml desiccated coconut

25 g flaked almonds

crème fraîche for serving

1. Place the chocolate and coconut oil in a glass bowl. Microwave on 50% power for 1 minute, then remove and stir until melted and smooth.

2. Pour the melted chocolate into a food processor with the cocoa powder, ground almonds, coconut flour, eggs, xylitol, almond butter, vanilla extract, baking powder and salt. Pulse until well combined.

3. Pour the mixture into a 16 × 25 cm lamington pan lined with baking paper and greased with nonstick cooking spray.

4. Sprinkle over the coconut and flaked almonds.

5. Bake in a preheated oven at 180°C for 20–25 minutes until a skewer inserted into the centre comes out clean. Remove from the oven and leave to cool in the pan for 5 minutes before cutting into squares. Serve warm with a dollop of crème fraîche.

Makes about 15 squares

Chocolate beetroot volcano puddings

3 eggs

60 ml castor sugar

60 g butter

200 g dark chocolate, chopped

60 ml beetroot purée (see below)

60 ml rice flour

pinch of salt

whipped cream for serving

1. In the bowl of an electric mixer, beat the eggs and castor sugar until pale and very thick.

2. Meanwhile, combine the butter and chocolate in a heatproof bowl and melt over a saucepan of simmering water.

3. Add the melted chocolate to the beaten eggs, together with the beetroot purée, rice flour and salt. Mix until combined.

4. Divide the mixture between 6 well-greased ramekins and place them on a baking tray.

5. Bake in a preheated oven at 180°C for 8–10 minutes. Test with a skewer; they should be soft in the middle.

6. Remove the puddings from the oven and leave to stand for about 5 minutes before turning out onto a plate or shallow pudding bowl. Serve with whipped cream.

Beetroot purée

1. Wash 1 large or 2 small beetroot. Place in a saucepan, cover with water and bring to the boil.

2. Simmer for 30–40 minutes until the beetroot is soft when pierced with a fork. Remove from the water and, when cool enough to handle, peel the beetroot and chop roughly.

3. Place the beetroot in a blender and purée, adding a little water, if necessary, to achieve a thick, smooth purée.

Makes 6

Christmas pudding with brandy sauce

This baked pudding is lighter than the traditional boiled version. Make it up to a week in advance and store, wrapped in cling wrap or foil, in an airtight container. The sauce can also be made ahead of time and stored, covered, in the refrigerator.

160 g dried fruit cake-mix
125 ml brandy
250 g dried pitted dates, chopped
250 ml boiling water
5 ml bicarbonate of soda
200 g butter
250 ml brown sugar

3 eggs
500 ml gluten-free self-raising flour
  (see page 8)
5 ml gluten-free mixed spice
5 ml gluten-free ground ginger
5 ml gluten-free ground cinnamon

Brandy sauce
250 ml cream
125 ml brown sugar
80 g butter
60 ml brandy
45 ml golden syrup

1. Combine the dried fruit cake-mix and brandy in a bowl and leave to soak for 30 minutes.
2. Put the dates in a separate bowl and pour over the boiling water. Add the bicarbonate of soda and stir well. Set aside to cool.
3. In another large bowl, cream the butter and brown sugar until light and fluffy.
4. Add the eggs, one at a time, beating after each addition.
5. Combine the gluten-free flour and spices. Add to the creamed mixture along with the dried fruit cake-mix and date mixtures. Mix until well combined.
6. Spoon the mixture into a well-greased 2-litre pudding basin. (If you don't have a pudding basin, use 2 loaf pans or a square cake pan instead.)
7. Bake in a preheated oven at 180°C for 40–50 minutes, or until a skewer inserted into the centre comes out clean. Remove from the oven and cool in the pan for 10 minutes before turning out onto a serving plate.
8. Serve with warm brandy sauce, plain custard or pouring cream.

Brandy sauce
1. Combine the ingredients in a small saucepan. Bring to the boil and cook for 1 minute, stirring occasionally.
2. Pour into a jug to serve. (If making ahead, leave to cool, then cover with cling wrap and refrigerate. Reheat gently before serving.)

Serves 8–10

Banoffee crumble pudding

If you're a fan of the inimitable toffee-banana tart, this variation should hit the right note.

125 g butter at room temperature, cubed
125 ml castor sugar
250 ml gluten-free flour (see page 8)
5 ml gluten-free baking powder
pinch of salt
2 eggs
5 ml vanilla essence

3–4 firm, ripe bananas, peeled and
  sliced on the diagonal
1 can (360 g) Nestlé Caramel Treat

Crumble
125 ml gluten-free flour (see page 8)
80 g butter

60 ml brown sugar
25 g pecan nuts, roughly chopped
60 ml gluten-free rolled oats
5 ml gluten-free ground cinnamon

1. Place the butter, castor sugar, gluten-free flour, baking powder, salt, eggs and vanilla essence into a food processor and blend to a thick and smooth batter.
2. Pour the batter into a deep 25 x 25 cm ovenproof dish that has been greased with nonstick cooking spray.
3. Layer the sliced bananas on top and spread with Caramel Treat.
4. Sprinkle the crumble over the caramel to cover.
5. Bake in a preheated oven at 180°C for 30–40 minutes until golden and bubbly. Serve warm.

Crumble

1. Place the gluten-free flour, butter and brown sugar into a food processor and blend to resemble breadcrumbs.
2. Add the rest of the ingredients and stir until combined.

Serves 4–6

Date and peanut squares

This recipe works equally well using almonds and almond butter in place of peanuts and peanut butter.
Adding a pinch of salt flakes makes these squares very moreish, but don't add extra salt if you use salted nuts.

200 g dried pitted dates,
   roughly chopped
200 g salted peanuts
160 ml dark chocolate chips

Topping
150 g dark chocolate, chopped
30 ml smooth peanut butter
40 g salted peanuts, chopped (optional)

1. Place the dates and peanuts in a food processor and pulse until finely chopped and well blended.
2. Add the chocolate chips and pulse until the mixture is thick and paste-like.
3. Press the mixture into a 18 x 23 cm baking tray lined with nonstick baking paper and smooth it with the back of a spoon. Refrigerate for a few hours until set.
4. Remove from the fridge and add the topping.
5. Cut into squares and store in an airtight container.

Topping

1. Melt the chocolate in the microwave and stir until smooth.
2. Stir in the peanut butter until well combined.
3. Spread the topping over the chilled date mixture. Sprinkle with chopped peanuts, if using.

Makes about 20 squares

Eggnog cheesecake

This cheesecake goes down a treat at Christmas. You can replace the brandy with any flavoured liqueur (Amarula is particularly good), or leave it out altogether if you prefer an alcohol-free dessert. Instead of the nut crust, you can use a gluten-free biscuit base (see Note, below).

Cinnamon nut crust

100 g pecan nuts, finely chopped

100 g blanched almonds, finely chopped

125 ml desiccated coconut

5 ml gluten-free ground cinnamon

25 ml xylitol or castor sugar

80–100 g butter or coconut oil, melted

Filling

3 tubs (250 g each) plain cream cheese

80 ml cream

60 ml brandy (optional)

180 ml xylitol or castor sugar

3 whole eggs

1 egg yolk

5 ml vanilla extract

grated nutmeg for topping

Crust

1. Combine the nuts, coconut, cinnamon and xylitol in a bowl and mix well.

2. Add enough melted butter to bind the mixture.

3. Press the mixture into the base of a 22-cm springform cake pan, levelling it with your fingertips. Place in the freezer for 10–15 minutes until firm.

4. Wrap the base and sides of the pan in a double layer of foil and place it inside a deep-sided roasting pan.

Filling

1. Beat the cream cheese, cream, brandy (if using) and xylitol in a bowl until smooth and creamy.

2. Beat in the eggs, egg yolk and vanilla extract. Pour over the crust in the prepared cake pan and grate some nutmeg on top.

3. Pour hot water into the roasting pan to come halfway up the sides of the cake pan.

4. Bake in a preheated oven at 160°C for 40–50 minutes until the edges are set and the centre still has a slight wobble. Switch off the oven, but leave the cheesecake inside for another hour to cool before removing from the oven. Take the cake pan out of the water and remove the foil. Refrigerate until chilled.

5. To serve, slide a flat-bladed knife around the edge of the cheesecake, then release the spring and remove the pan. Slide a knife under the crust to loosen it from the base and slide the cheesecake onto a serving plate. Refrigerate until required. (It is important to remove the cheesecake from the springform pan as soon as it has chilled. Leaving it overnight will result in the sides of the cheesecake becoming discoloured from the metal of the pan.)

Serves 8–10

Note *To make a biscuit base, replace the nuts with 200 g crushed gluten-free biscuits mixed with 100 g melted butter.*

Dairy-free strawberry tart

Crust

1 quantity gluten-free shortcrust pastry
   (see page 148)

Filling

2 eggs, beaten
60 ml cornflour
50 ml xylitol or castor sugar
30 ml custard powder

250 ml coconut milk
250 ml coconut cream
1 vanilla pod, seeds removed
250 g halved strawberries for serving
60 ml smooth apricot jam for glazing

Crust

1. Roll out the chilled pastry between 2 sheets of nonstick baking paper to a 5 mm thickness and line
   a 23-cm quiche pan or pie plate.
2. Prick the base, line with nonstick baking paper and fill with dried beans.
3. Bake blind in a preheated oven at 160°C for 15–20 minutes until pale golden brown. Remove the paper and beans
   and return to the oven for another 5 minutes to finish drying out and baking the crust. Leave to cool before adding the filling.

Filling

1. Combine the eggs, cornflour, xylitol and custard powder in a bowl. Add half the coconut milk and mix until smooth.
2. Place the remaining coconut milk, coconut cream and vanilla seeds in a saucepan and heat until just boiling.
3. Pour the hot mixture into the cornflour mixture, stirring constantly.
4. Return the mixture to the saucepan and cook over a low heat until thickened.
5. Remove from the heat and pour the warm mixture into the cooled pastry shell. Smooth the top and leave to cool.
6. Arrange the halved strawberries on top. Warm the apricot jam and brush it over the strawberries, to glaze.

Serves 12–14

Note *Rolling the delicate pastry between 2 sheets of nonstick baking paper makes it easier to handle.*

Baking

Low-carb fruit and nut loaf

250 ml sunflower seed meal
  (see Note, below)
125 ml coconut flour
50 g ground almonds
30 ml psyllium husks

125 ml xylitol
15 ml gluten-free baking powder
10 ml gluten-free ground cinnamon
5 ml gluten-free ground ginger
80 g butter, melted

3 eggs
200 ml double cream (Greek) yoghurt
75 g dried cranberries, chopped
50 g pecan nuts, chopped

1. Combine the sunflower seed meal, coconut flour, ground almonds, psyllium husks, xylitol, baking powder and ground spices in a large bowl.
2. In another bowl, mix together the melted butter, eggs and yoghurt and beat well.
3. Add the butter mixture to the dry ingredients and mix until well combined.
4. Stir in the cranberries and pecan nuts.
5. Spoon the mixture into a small loaf pan that has been greased and lined with nonstick baking paper.
6. Bake in a preheated oven at 180°C for 40–50 minutes, or until a skewer inserted into the centre comes out clean. Remove from the oven and leave to cool in the pan for 5 minutes before transferring to a cooling rack.

Makes 1 loaf

Note *To make 250 ml sunflower seed meal (flour), place ± 150 g sunflower seeds in a coffee grinder or mini blender and process until finely ground.*

Apple and cranberry crumble squares

Crumble

250 g butter

250 g castor sugar

750 ml gluten-free flour mix (see page 8)

5 ml gluten-free baking powder

Apple and cranberry filling

1 can (400 g) pie apples

90 g dried cranberries

60 ml castor sugar

zest and juice of 1 lemon

50 g chopped pecan nuts for garnishing

Crumble

1. Cream the butter and castor sugar in a bowl until very light and fluffy.

2. Add the gluten-free flour mix and baking powder and mix to form a crumbly texture.

3. Divide the mixture in half. Press half of the mixture into a 20 x 30 cm baking tray that has been greased and lined with nonstick baking paper.

Filling

1. Combine the apples, dried cranberries, castor sugar, lemon zest and lemon juice in a bowl.

2. Spread the filling evenly over the crumble base.

3. Sprinkle over the remaining crumble and scatter with the chopped pecan nuts.

4. Bake in a preheated oven at 180°C for 40–50 minutes until both the base and the topping are golden brown. Remove from the oven and leave to cool in the pan before cutting into squares.

Makes 25–30 small squares

Light fruit cake

150 g butter

180 ml castor sugar

2 eggs

5 ml orange extract

zest of 1 orange

zest of 1 lemon

375 ml gluten-free self-raising flour

   (see Note below, or page 8)

5 ml xanthan gum

200 g dried fruit cake-mix

100 g glacé cherries, halved

100 g mixed peel

30 ml brandy (optional)

1. Cream the butter and castor sugar in a large bowl until light and fluffy.

2. Add the eggs, one at a time, beating after each addition.

3. Mix in the orange extract, orange rind and lemon rind.

4. Add the gluten-free self-raising flour and xanthan gum and mix to combine.

5. Finally stir in the dried fruit cake-mix, cherries, mixed peel and brandy, if using.

6. Line the base of a 11 x 20 cm loaf pan with nonstick baking paper and spray with nonstick cooking spray.
    Spoon the mixture into the pan.

7. Bake in a preheated oven at 160°C for 40–50 minutes, or until a skewer inserted into the centre comes out clean.
    (If the top of the cake starts getting too dark, cover it with a piece of foil.) Remove and cool in the pan for 10 minutes before
    turning out onto a cooling rack.

Makes 1 loaf cake

Note *To make self-raising flour, add 5 ml baking powder for every 250 ml flour called for.*

Cheese and herb scones

750 ml gluten-free flour mix (see page 8)
100 g butter
375 ml grated Cheddar cheese
60 ml finely chopped fresh chives

60 ml finely chopped fresh parsley
salt ground black pepper to taste
2 eggs
200 ml milk

5 ml gluten-free prepared mustard
 (optional)
rice flour or cornflour for dusting
1 beaten egg for brushing

1. Place the gluten-free flour mix in a mixing bowl. Add the butter and rub it in with your fingertips to resemble breadcrumbs.
2. Stir in the Cheddar cheese and herbs. Season with salt and pepper.
3. In a jug, whisk together the 2 eggs, milk and mustard, if using.
4. Add the egg mixture to the flour mixture and mix with a fork just until the mixture comes together. Do not overmix.
5. Sprinkle the work surface with rice flour or cornflour. Place the scone mixture on the floured surface and roll out to 5 cm thick.
    Cut out rounds with a cookie cutter and place them on a baking tray sprayed with nonstick cooking spray.
    Brush with the beaten egg.
6. Bake in a preheated oven at 200°C for 15–20 minutes until golden. Serve with extra grated cheese, if desired.

Makes 12

Low-carb seed bread

250 ml almond flour
180 ml coconut flour
60 ml psyllium husks
125 ml mixed seeds

5 ml salt
15 ml baking powder
5 eggs
250 g cream cheese

180 ml buttermilk
80 ml melted coconut oil
extra seeds for sprinkling

1. Combine the almond flour, coconut flour, psyllium husks, seeds, salt and baking powder in a bowl.
2. Using an electric mixer, beat together the eggs, cream cheese and buttermilk until smooth. Beat in the coconut oil.
3. Add the egg mixture to the dry ingredients and mix well.
4. Spoon the mixture into a lined and greased 11 x 18 cm loaf pan. Sprinkle the top with extra seeds.
5. Bake in a preheated oven at 180°C for 40–50 minutes, or until a skewer inserted into the centre of the loaf comes out clean.
    The crust should be crisp and the loaf should sound hollow when tapped.

Makes 1 medium loaf

Seed crunchies

250 g butter

15 ml golden syrup

500 ml gluten-free rolled oats

250 ml sugar or xylitol

5 ml bicarbonate of soda

250 ml desiccated coconut

250 ml gluten-free flour mix (see page 8)

250 ml mixed seeds

1. Melt the butter and golden syrup in a small saucepan.
2. Combine the dry ingredients in a bowl.
3. Add the melted butter and mix well.
4. Press the mixture firmly into a greased 30 x 20 cm baking tray.
5. Bake in a preheated oven at 180°C for 15–20 minutes, until golden brown.
   Remove from the oven and leave to cool slightly in the baking tray before cutting into fingers or squares.

Makes about 30

Cheese biscuits

These are perfect for a cheese board, accompanied by gherkins and onion marmalade.

375 ml gluten-free flour (see page 8)

5 ml gluten-free baking powder

5 ml salt

10 ml mixed dried herbs

125 g butter, cubed

100 g Cheddar cheese, grated

1 egg

1 egg white, lightly whisked

sesame seeds for sprinkling

1. Sift the gluten-free flour, baking powder and salt into the bowl of a food processor.
2. Add the mixed herbs and butter, and pulse to resemble breadcrumbs.
3. Add the Cheddar cheese and pulse to combine.
4. Add the egg and pulse until the mixture forms a ball.
5. Remove and knead slightly. Wrap in cling wrap and refrigerate for 30 minutes.
6. Divide the dough in half. On a flour-dusted surface, roll out one half of the dough to about 3 mm thickness and cut out rounds using a cookie cutter. Repeat with the second half of the dough.
7. Arrange the rounds on a baking tray. Prick the rounds with a fork, lightly brush with the egg white and sprinkle with sesame seeds.
8. Bake in a preheated oven at 180°C for 10–15 minutes until golden. Leave the biscuits to cool on the baking tray. Store in an airtight container.

Makes about 40

Cinnamon angel food cake

This recipe works best if made in a special chiffon cake pan, which has extended legs onto which the pan is inverted when it comes out of the oven. This allows the cake to hang while it is cooling. If you turn the cake out while it is still hot it will collapse into itself and have a dense, heavy texture.

250 ml gluten-free flour mix (see page 8)
200 ml castor sugar
60 ml cornflour
5 ml gluten-free ground cinnamon
5 ml xanthan gum
10 egg whites (300 ml)

7 ml cream of tartar
125 ml extra castor sugar
7 ml vanilla essence
fresh raspberries for decorating

Spiced cream
250 ml cream
60 ml castor sugar
3 ml gluten-free ground cinnamon

1. Sift together the gluten-free flour, castor sugar, cornflour, cinnamon and xanthan gum.
2. Beat the egg whites with the cream of tartar in a large bowl until soft peaks form.
3. Gradually beat in the extra castor sugar until the mixture is thick. Beat in the vanilla essence.
4. Add the flour in 2 batches, using a large metal spoon to fold it in carefully.
5. Spoon the mixture into an ungreased chiffon pan and bake in a preheated oven at 180°C for 30–40 minutes, or until a skewer inserted into the centre comes out clean.
6. Remove the pan from the oven, invert it and leave to cool completely. Carefully loosen the cake from the sides of the pan and turn out onto a serving plate. Cover with the spiced cream and decorate with fresh raspberries.

Spiced cream
1. Beat the cream, castor sugar and cinnamon until stiff.

Makes 1 cake

Biscotti with almonds and cranberries

375 ml gluten-free flour mix (see page 8)	10 ml lemon zest	3 eggs, beaten
180 ml castor sugar	5 ml xanthan gum	80 ml melted coconut oil
100 g ground almonds	150 g dried cranberries, roughly chopped	(see Note, below)
10 ml gluten-free baking powder	50 g flaked almonds	3 ml almond extract

1. Combine the gluten-free flour, castor sugar, ground almonds, baking powder, lemon zest and xanthan gum in a large bowl and mix well.
2. Add the cranberries and flaked almonds and mix.
3. In a separate bowl, combine the eggs, coconut oil and almond extract and mix.
4. Add the egg mixture to the dry ingredients and mix to make a dough that is slightly soft, but not sticky.
5. Divide the dough in half. Form each half into a log shape roughly 20 cm long and 4 cm thick. Place on a baking tray lined with baking paper.
6. Bake in a preheated oven at 180°C for 20–30 minutes, or until a skewer inserted into the centre comes out clean. Remove from the oven and leave to cool completely.
7. Using a serrated knife, cut the logs into 6-mm-thin slices, laying the slices flat on a baking tray.
8. Lower the oven temperature to 160°C. Return the biscotti to the oven and bake for 10–15 minutes, until pale golden on both sides (turn the biscotti halfway through the cooking time). Store in an airtight container.

Makes 20–24

Note *You can replace the coconut oil with melted butter. Deflavoured coconut oil is best, as it has a neutral flavour that won't clash with other flavours in the recipe.*

Cinnamon buns

These are best eaten warm, fresh out of the oven.

Cinnamon-sugar filling

100 g butter, softened

160 ml castor sugar

20 ml gluten-free ground cinnamon

Dough

500 ml gluten-free flour mix (*see* page 8)

5 ml salt

15 ml baking powder

5 ml xanthan gum

30 ml sugar

80 g butter, cubed

1 egg

180 ml buttermilk

Glaze

125 ml icing sugar

water to mix

a few drops vanilla essence

Filling

1. Cream together the butter, castor sugar and cinnamon in a bowl. Set aside.

Dough

1. Combine the gluten-free flour, salt, baking powder, xanthan gum and sugar in a bowl.

2. Add the butter and rub it in until the mixture resembles breadcrumbs.

3. In a separate bowl, combine the egg and buttermilk and mix well. Add to the flour mixture and mix gently to bring the dough together.

4. Turn the dough out onto a floured surface and knead gently.

5. Roll the dough into a 20 x 30 cm rectangle. Spread with the cinnamon-sugar mixture.

6. Working from the long side, roll up the dough to form a sausage shape.

7. Cut the dough roll into 12 slices. Place each slice, cut-side up, in a well-greased muffin pan.

8. Bake in a preheated oven at 180°C for 20 minutes, or until golden brown. Remove from the oven and leave the buns to cool in the pan for 5 minutes before carefully removing. When cool, drizzle each bun with some glaze.

Glaze

1. Sift the icing sugar into a bowl and add enough water to make a thick glaze. Stir in the vanilla essence.

Makes 12

Carrot cake

For a special occasion, decorate this perennial tea-time favourite with pecan nuts and chopped dried fruit.

4 extra large eggs

250 ml castor sugar

180 ml sunflower oil

500 ml gluten-free flour mix (see page 8)

5 ml xanthan gum

10 ml bicarbonate of soda

10 ml gluten-free ground cinnamon

5 ml salt

750 ml coarsely grated carrots

50 g pecan nuts, chopped, optional

extra chopped pecan nuts or
toasted flaked almonds for decorating

Cream cheese icing

80 g butter

125 g thick cream cheese

5 ml vanilla essence

500 ml icing sugar, sifted

1. Beat the eggs and castor sugar in a bowl until thick and pale.
2. Beat in the sunflower oil.
3. Sift together the gluten-free flour, xanthan gum, bicarbonate of soda, cinnamon and salt and stir into the egg mixture.
4. Fold in the grated carrots and pecan nuts, if using.
5. Spoon the mixture into a 23-cm ring pan or 2 loaf pans (22 x 12 cm) sprayed with nonstick cooking spray.
   Bake in a preheated oven at 160°C for 50–60 minutes, or until a skewer inserted into the cake comes out clean.

Icing

1. Cream the butter and cream cheese until smooth.
2. Add the vanilla essence and icing sugar and beat to make a thick, fluffy icing. Spread over the cooled cake.
   Decorate with chopped pecans or flaked almonds and/or lemon zest, if desired.

Makes 1 ring cake or 2 loaf cakes

Lemon polenta cake

180 g butter

250 ml castor sugar

3 eggs

200 g ground almonds

150 ml polenta

5 ml gluten-free baking powder

pinch of salt

30 ml lemon juice

zest of 1 large lemon

Syrup

45 ml lemon juice

30 ml icing sugar, plus extra for dusting

1. Cream the butter and castor sugar in a bowl until light and fluffy. Add the eggs, one at a time, beating after each addition.
2. Mix in the ground almonds, polenta, baking powder and salt.
3. Fold in the lemon juice and rind.
4. Pour the mixture into a greased and lined 20-cm square pan.
5. Bake in a preheated oven at 180°C for 40–50 minutes, or until a skewer inserted into the centre comes out clean. (If the cake starts to brown too quickly, cover the top with a piece of foil.) Remove from the oven and brush over the lemon syrup.

Syrup

1. Combine the lemon juice and icing sugar in a heatproof bowl and microwave on full power for 1 minute.

Makes 1 cake

Lemon loaf

125 g butter, softened

180 ml castor sugar

2 extra large eggs

375 ml gluten-free flour mix (see page 8)

5 ml xanthan gum

10 ml baking powder

125 ml milk

15 ml finely grated lemon zest, plus extra

Lemon icing

250 ml icing sugar, sifted

20 ml lemon juice

water to mix

1. Cream the butter and castor sugar well in a large bowl. Add the eggs, one at a time, beating after each addition.
2. Sift the dry ingredients and add to the creamed mixture alternately with the milk. Mix through the lemon zest.
3. Spoon the mixture into a greased and lined 23 x 13 cm loaf pan.
4. Bake in a preheated oven at 180°C for 40–45 minutes, or until a skewer inserted into the centre comes out clean. Remove from the oven and leave in the pan for 10 minutes before turning out onto a rack. Allow to cool completely before icing.

Lemon icing

1. Combine the icing sugar, lemon juice and a little water to make a thick, but still runny, icing. Drizzle over the cake and decorate with extra lemon zest or thin strips of rind.

Makes 1 loaf cake

Rusks

4 × 250 ml gluten-free flour mix
(see page 8)
250 g butter, cubed
375 ml light brown sugar
250 ml desiccated coconut

100 g ground almonds
100 g sesame seeds
60 ml psyllium husks
20 ml baking powder
5 ml bicarbonate of soda

5 ml salt
500 g double-cream (Greek) yoghurt
4 eggs

1. Put the gluten-free flour mix into a large bowl.
2. Rub in the butter until the mixture resembles breadcrumbs.
3. Add the sugar, coconut, ground almonds, sesame seeds, psyllium husks, baking powder, bicarbonate of soda and salt. Mix well.
4. Combine the yoghurt and eggs in a separate bowl and mix well. Add to the dry ingredients and mix to form a stiff batter.
5. Spoon the batter into a greased 30 × 40 cm baking tray. Use wet hands to smooth the top.
6. Bake in a preheated oven at 180°C for 25–30 minutes, or until a skewer inserted into the centre comes out clean.
    Leave to cool in the tray, then turn out and cut into fingers.
7. Place the rusks on a clean baking tray. Lower the oven temperature to 50°C and dry the rusks for 6–8 hours, or overnight.
    Store in an airtight container.

Makes 50–60

Sponge fingers

These are perfect for making tiramisu.

3 eggs, separated
80 ml castor sugar, plus extra
   for sprinkling

60 ml gluten-free flour mix (see page 8)
60 ml cornflour
1 ml salt

5 ml vanilla extract

1. Place the egg whites into the bowl of an electric mixer or food processor and whisk until soft peaks form. Gradually add the castor sugar, beating well after each addition. The mixture should be glossy.
2. In another bowl, whisk the egg yolks with a fork.
3. In a third bowl, sift the gluten-free flour mix, cornflour and salt.
4. Keeping the mixer on a low speed, fold the yolks and flour alternately into the whites, scraping down the sides of the bowl as necessary. Stir in the vanilla extract.
5. Transfer the mixture to a piping bag fitted with a 1.5 cm nozzle. Pipe 8-cm-long fingers onto 2 baking trays lined with nonstick baking paper, leaving space between each. Sprinkle with extra castor sugar.
6. Bake in a preheated oven at 180°C for 20–25 minutes. Remove the fingers from the oven and cool on the tray for 5 minutes before transfering to a wire rack to cool completely. Store in an airtight container.

Makes 20

Almond & orange Florentines

125 ml sugar

80 ml cream

60 g butter

200 g ground almonds

60 ml orange marmalade

45 ml gluten-free flour mix (see page 8)

5 ml vanilla extract

5 ml finely grated orange zest

2 ml salt flakes

melted dark chocolate, for drizzling

1. Place the sugar, cream and butter in a saucepan. Bring to the boil and cook, stirring, until the mixture begins to brown.

2. Remove from the heat and stir in the ground almonds, marmalade, gluten-free flour, vanilla extract, orange zest and salt flakes.

3. Drop teaspoonfuls onto a baking tray lined with baking paper. When cool enough to handle, use damp fingers to press each disc flat.

4. Bake in a preheated oven at 160°C for 15–20 minutes until dark golden. Remove and cool completely before drizzling with melted dark chocolate.

Makes 14–16

Ginger orange cake

125 ml orange juice

70 g sultanas

250 ml coconut flour

125 ml tapioca flour

125 ml icing sugar

5 ml gluten-free baking powder

3 ml bicarbonate of soda

2 ml salt

10 ml gluten-free ground ginger

5 ml gluten-free ground cinnamon

2 ml gluten-free ground cloves

180 ml molasses

125 ml buttermilk

60 ml sunflower oil

10 ml grated orange zest

3 eggs

1. Place the orange juice and sultanas in a small saucepan. Bring to the boil, then remove from the heat. Set aside and leave to cool.

2. Sift the dry ingredients into a medium bowl.

3. Combine the rest of the ingredients in a separate bowl and whisk together well with a hand beater until foamy.

4. Add the dry mixture to the molasses-buttermilk mixture and beat until just combined.

5. Pour off any excess liquid from the sultanas and fold them into the mixture. Leave the batter to stand for 10 minutes, then pour into a greased 23-cm ring pan. (To make it easier, pour the batter into a jug first, or use a ladle.)

6. Bake in a preheated oven at 180°C for 50–60 minutes until a skewer inserted into the cake comes out clean. Remove from the oven and cool in the pan for 10 minutes before turning out onto a rack to cool completely.

Makes 1 ring cake

Mocha cake

200 g dark chocolate, chopped
25 ml coffee powder
250 ml boiling water
10 ml vanilla essence
200 g butter
375 ml castor sugar

3 eggs
500 ml gluten-free flour mix (see page 8)
5 ml gluten-free baking powder
5 ml bicarbonate of soda
5 ml xanthan gum

Coffee icing
250 ml sifted icing sugar
30 ml ready-made strong coffee

1. Put the chocolate into a heatproof bowl.
2. Dissolve the coffee powder in the boiling water and add the vanilla essence. Pour this over the chocolate and set aside, stirring occasionally, until the chocolate has melted.
3. Cream the butter and castor sugar very well in a large bowl until light and creamy.
4. Add the eggs, one at a time, beating well after each addition.
5. Sift the gluten-free flour, baking powder, bicarbonate of soda and xanthan gum. Add to the creamed mixture alternately with the chocolate-coffee mixture.
6. Spoon into a well-greased 20-cm ring pan. Bake in a preheated oven at 180°C for 40–50 minutes, or until a skewer inserted into the cake comes out clean. Remove from the oven and cool in the pan for 10 minutes before turning out onto a wire rack. When the cake is cold, drizzle with the icing.

Icing
1. Mix the icing sugar with enough coffee to make a thick, but still runny icing.

Makes 1 ring cake

Vanilla cupcakes

125 g butter, softened
250 ml castor sugar
3 eggs
7 ml vanilla essence
500 ml gluten-free flour mix (see page 8)
7 ml gluten-free baking powder

2 ml bicarbonate of soda
pinch of salt
200–250 ml buttermilk

Butter icing
125 g butter
625 ml icing sugar
milk or water to mix
5 ml vanilla essence
food colouring (optional)

1. Cream the butter and castor sugar in a large bowl until light and fluffy.
2. Add the eggs, one at a time, beating well after each addition. Add the vanilla essence.
3. Sift the dry ingredients into a second bowl.
4. Add the dry ingredients to the creamed mixture alternately with enough buttermilk to make a soft, dropping consistency.
5. Spoon the mixture into paper-lined muffin cups (use two 12-cup muffin or cupcake pans).
6. Bake in a preheated oven at 180°C for 15–20 minutes. Remove and leave to cool before icing.

Icing

1. Cream the butter until soft.
2. Sift the icing sugar into the creamed butter. Mix well to combine.
3. Add just enough milk or water to obtain a spreadable consistency.
4. Add the vanilla essence and a few drops of food colouring (if using) and stir through.

Makes about 18

Melting moments

200 g butter, softened

160 ml icing sugar

5 ml vanilla extract

125 ml gluten-free custard powder

400 ml gluten-free flour mix (see page 8)

1. In a bowl, cream the butter and icing sugar well.
2. Mix in the vanilla extract.
3. Add the custard powder and gluten-free flour and mix to form a stiff dough.
4. Roll the dough into balls the size of a walnut and place on a greased baking tray. Press each ball flat with a fork.
5. Bake in a preheated oven at 160°C for 15–20 minutes until pale golden.
   Remove from the oven and leave to cool on the tray.

Makes 16—18

Chocolate biscuits

125 g butter
125 ml brown sugar
1 egg
5 ml vanilla essence

180 ml gluten-free flour mix (see page 8)
125 ml cocoa powder
3 ml bicarbonate of soda
2.5 ml xanthan gum

250 ml white chocolate chips

1. Beat the butter and brown sugar together in a bowl until creamy.

2. Beat in the egg and vanilla essence.

3. Sift together the gluten-free flour, cocoa powder, bicarbonate of soda and xanthan gum. Beat into the creamed mixture. Add the chocolate chips and fold in.

4. Roll rounded tablespoons of the dough into balls. Place on a baking sheet lined with baking paper and sprayed with nonstick cooking spray. Use the palm of your hand to flatten each ball slightly.

5. Bake in a preheated oven at 180°C for 10–15 minutes. Remove from the oven and leave to cool on the baking sheet for 5 minutes before transferring to a wire rack.

Makes 20

Chocolate loaf

180 g butter

125 ml castor sugar

4 eggs, separated

100 g dark chocolate, melted
   and cooled slightly

250 ml gluten-free flour mix (see page 8)

10 ml baking powder

60 ml cocoa powder

50 g ground almonds

60 ml extra castor sugar

Chocolate glaze

200 g dark chocolate, chopped

100 ml cream

1. Cream the butter and castor sugar in a bowl until light and fluffy.
2. Add the egg yolks and beat well.
3. Beat in the cooled melted chocolate.
4. Sift the gluten-free flour, baking powder and cocoa powder and fold into the creamed mixture.
5. Fold in the ground almonds.
6. In a separate bowl, beat the egg whites until stiff, then gradually beat in the extra castor sugar.
   Fold the egg white mixture into the chocolate mixture.
7. Spoon the mixture into a 13 x 23-cm loaf pan lined and sprayed with nonstick cooking spray.
8. Bake in a preheated oven at 180°C for 40–50 minutes, or until a skewer inserted into the centre comes out clean.
   Remove and cool in the pan for 10 minutes before turning out onto a wire rack. When completely cool, spread
   with the chocolate glaze.

Glaze

1. Combine the chocolate and cream in a bowl and microwave on 50% power for 1–2 minutes until melted.
2. Stir until smooth, then leave to cool until the mixture is spreadable.
3. Spread on top of the cooled cake and decorate as desired.

Makes 1 loaf cake

Cardamom shortbread

125 g butter at room temperature, cubed

125 ml xylitol or castor sugar

125 ml potato flour

125 ml cornflour

125 ml rice flour

50 g ground almonds

15 ml ground cardamom

5 ml vanilla extract

1. Place all the ingredients into a food processor and blend until a dough forms.
2. Press the dough evenly into a 20-cm-square baking pan that has been lightly sprayed with nonstick cooking spray.
3. Bake in a preheated oven at 150°C for 40–50 minutes, or until just golden. Remove from the oven and leave to cool in the pan before cutting into squares or fingers. Store in an airtight container.

Makes 16 squares

Nutty biscuit treats

125 ml macadamia nut butter

125 ml light brown sugar

1 egg

250 ml chickpea flour

250 ml brown rice flour

50 g ground almonds

5 ml bicarbonate of soda

80–100 ml coconut milk

extra ground almonds for sprinkling

1. Cream together the macadamia nut butter and light brown sugar in a bowl.
2. Add the egg and mix well.
3. Add the flours, ground almonds and bicarbonate of soda and combine with enough coconut milk to make a dough that is slightly soft, but not too sticky.
4. Roll spoonfuls of the mixture into balls and place on a greased baking tray. Flatten each ball with your hand. Sprinkle each biscuit with a little extra ground almonds, pressing them in with your fingertips.
5. Bake in a preheated oven at 180°C for 10–15 minutes, until the biscuits are golden brown underneath.

Makes 20–30

Note: *You can replace the coconut milk with buttermilk, if preferred.*

Banana coconut cake

375 ml gluten-free flour mix (see page 8)

150 ml polenta

5 ml gluten-free baking powder

5 ml xanthan gum

3 eggs

375 ml sugar

125 ml canola or sunflower oil

3 bananas, mashed

80 ml milk

5 ml vanilla essence

125 ml desiccated coconut

coconut flakes for decorating

Cream cheese icing

80 g butter, softened

125 g block cream cheese

500 ml icing sugar, sifted

5 ml vanilla essence

1. Sift the gluten-free flour, polenta, baking powder and xanthan gum into a bowl.

2. In a separate bowl, beat the eggs and sugar with an electric mixer until thick and pale. Beat in the oil.

3. Combine the bananas, milk and vanilla essence.

4. Add the banana mixture to the egg mixture alternately with the sifted dry ingredients. Fold in the desiccated coconut.

5. Pour the mixture into a greased and lined 20-cm round cake pan.

6. Bake in a preheated oven at 160°C for 60–70 minutes, or until a skewer inserted into the centre comes out clean. (If the cake is starting to get too brown, cover it with foil.) Remove from the oven and leave to cool in the pan for 10 minutes before turning out onto a rack to cool completely.

7. When cold, spread the top of the cake with icing and sprinkle with coconut flakes.

Icing

1. Cream the butter and cream cheese in a bowl until light and fluffy.

2. Beat in the icing sugar and vanilla essence to make a spreadable icing.

Makes 1 cake

Note *For added colour, toast the coconut flakes in a dry pan until the edges turn golden-brown, taking care not to burn them.*

Red velvet cupcakes

125 g butter, softened

250 ml castor sugar

2 eggs

300 ml gluten-free flour mix (see page 8)

60 ml cocoa powder

5 ml bicarbonate of soda

5 ml xanthan gum

pinch of salt

125 ml buttermilk

15 ml red food colouring

5 ml white vinegar

cocoa powder, for dusting, optional

Cream cheese icing

80 g butter, softened

125 g block cream cheese

500 ml icing sugar, sifted

5 ml vanilla essence

1. Cream the butter and castor sugar in a bowl until light and fluffy.

2. Beat in the eggs, one at a time.

3. Sift together the gluten-free flour, cocoa powder, bicarbonate of soda, xanthan gum and salt.

4. Mix together the buttermilk, red food colouring and vinegar.

5. Add the flour to the creamed mixture alternately with the buttermilk until well blended.

6. Spoon the mixture into a 12-cup muffin pan lined with paper liners.

7. Bake in a preheated oven at 160°C for 25–30 minutes, or until a skewer inserted into the centre of a cupcake comes out clean.
   Remove from the pan and leave to cool on a wire rack. When cool, spread or pipe cream cheese icing onto each cupcake.
   Dust with extra cocoa powder or add some sprinkles, if desired.

Icing

1. Cream the butter and cream cheese in a bowl until light and fluffy.

2. Beat in the icing sugar and vanilla essence to make a spreadable icing.

Makes 12

Gluten-free shortcrust pastry

500 ml gluten-free flour mix (see page 8)
pinch of salt
5 ml xanthan gum

160 g butter, cut into small pieces
grated zest of 1 lemon
125 ml icing sugar

1 egg
30–40 ml iced water

1. Combine the flour mix, salt, xanthan gum, butter, lemon zest and icing sugar in a food processor and whizz to form crumbs.
2. Add the egg and iced water, and pulse to form a dough (do not overmix; add a little extra water if necessary). Wrap in cling wrap and chill in the fridge for 20–30 minutes.

Note *This pastry is quite delicate. To make it easier to handle when rolling out, place the dough between 2 sheets of nonstick baking paper.*

Traditional fruit mince pies

Filling
425–450 g fruit mince
70–75 g dried cranberries
50 g slivered almonds, lightly toasted
finely grated zest and juice of 1 orange
50 ml brandy (optional)

beaten egg for glazing
castor sugar for sifting

1 quantity gluten-free shortcrust pastry
  (see above)

1. To make the filling, place the fruit mince, cranberries, almonds, orange zest and juice, and brandy, if using, into a small saucepan and bring to the boil. Simmer for a few minutes, then set aside to cool completely.
2. Remove the chilled pastry from the fridge and divide it in half. Roll out one half of the pastry to about 5 mm thick and cut out discs to fit the patty pan cups (see Note). Place a heaped teaspoon of fruit mince into each pastry case, but don't overfill.
3. Roll out the remaining dough, and any offcuts, to about 5 mm thick. Stamp out star shapes as lids, then place the lids on the pies, moistening the edges with water, if necessary, to attach the lid to the pastry case.
4. Brush the pastry stars with beaten egg. Bake in a preheated oven at 180°C for 12–15 minutes, or until the pastry is light golden brown. Remove from the oven and sift over some castor sugar. Cool in the tray for 5 minutes, then remove the mince pies and place on a wire rack until cold.

Note *You need shallow patty pan (tartlet) trays and a star-shaped cutter for this recipe. If you don't have 2 trays, you can make the mince pies in batches.*

Makes 18

Index

Conversion table

Metric	Imperial
Millilitres	Teaspoons
2 ml	¼ tsp
3 ml	½ tsp
5 ml	1 tsp
10 ml	2 tsp
20 ml	4 tsp
Millilitres	Tablespoons
15 ml	1 Tbsp
30 ml	2 Tbsp
45 ml	3 Tbsp
Millilitres	Cups
60 ml	¼ cup
80 ml	⅓ cup
125 ml	½ cup
160 ml	⅔ cup
200 ml	¾ cup
250 ml	1 cup
375 ml	1½ cups
500 ml	2 cups
1 litre	4 cups